DHARMA IF YOU DARE

Dharma If You Dare

Living Life with Abandon

QAPEL DOUG DUNCAN

Edited by Laura Bean and Linda Yamashita

Dharma If You Dare: Living Life with Abandon
by Doug Duncan

Planet Dharma
3567 Cockell Road
Fort Steele, British Columbia
V0B 1N0 Canada
publishing@planetdharma.com

© 2013, 2017, 2020, 2023 Doug Duncan

ISBN-13: 978-0-9985886-0-5

This work is licensed under the Creative Commons Attribution-ShareAlike 4.0 International License. To view a copy of this license, visit http://creativecommons.org/licenses/by-sa/4.0/ or send a letter to Creative Commons, PO Box 1866, Mountain View, CA 94042, USA.

Library and Archives Canada Cataloguing in Publication: on p. ix
Duncan, Doug, 1949-
    Dharma if you dare : living life with abandon / by Doug Duncan ; edited by Laura Bean and Linda Yamashita
ISBN 978-0-9917701-0-6
    1. Religious life--Buddhism. 2. Buddhism--Doctrines.
I. Title.
BQ4302.D85 2013   294.3'444   C2013-900975-2

In memory of

THE VENERABLE NAMGYAL RINPOCHE

*May the unbroken line of guides continue
to expect the very best of us*

CONTENTS

Acknowledgments		i
Introduction		iii
Namo Tassa Bhagavato Arahato Samma Sambuddhassa		v
1	Beautifully Bent Trees and the Forest of Emptiness: Rediscovering your true nature	1
2	Absorption 101: Befriending the meditation cushion	11
3	600 Tubes of Toothpaste: Creativity and karma	21
4	Big Rocks: Discovering your purpose	33
5	Living Well, Letting Go: Four principles of spiritual development	45
6	The Hungry Ego: Creating space between yourself and your objects	57
7	The Keys to the Palace: The five faculties and five hindrances	67
8	Fishing in Deep Waters: Acknowledging the shadows	79
9	Docking the QE II: Instructions for meditation retreat	87
10	Nuts and Bolts of Practice: The four foundations of mindfulness	99
11	Magic Carpet Ride: Coming to trust	105

ACKNOWLEDGMENTS

Our Japan Sangha was the maternal nest of these teachings and this project. Many hearts and minds contributed to it. The transcribers included Robert Blaisdell, Duncan Cryle, Hon Tong "Bat" Fung, Tim Newfields, Todd Stewart, and Andrea Netscher. The team of editors who helped get the project off the ground was made up of Lisa Feder, Ursula Maierl, Kim Mangialaschi, and Peter Ujlaki. Renata Drtina, John Munroe, and Richard Sadowsky helped with final editing and proofreading. David Rogers and Karen McAllister were responsible for the layout, and Donna Kellison created the cover design. Michael Hofmann provided the inside illustrations. Special thanks to Susan Fisher, who edited an individual chapter and helped finish the manuscript, and to Karen McAllister for her eleventh-hour technical assistance. To everyone who gave of themselves to realize this project we are humbly grateful. Last but not least, profound gratitude to Catherine Pawasarat Sensei for steadfastly supporting and promoting these teachings, and to Qapel Doug Duncan for the precious gift of the Dharma.

Laura Bean and Linda Yamashita

INTRODUCTION

I've always loved the title, *Dharma If You Dare*. Even before I got to read a single page from the book, for me it resonated with what drew me to Qapel Doug Duncan as a teacher, and to the Namgyal lineage in general. Although being around Qapel's warm, joyful, down-to-earth energy always felt nourishing and healing to be around, there was also always a sense of danger: this was someone whose mandate was clearly to help me break free of my limited, habitual views of the world.

In the 10 years since I saw the first box of *Dare* copies opened at the Clear Sky Retreat Center offices, I've reflected a lot about the title of the book. While the title resonated with me intuitively, and sections of the book–like Chapter 5 on the Challenges–seem to speak directly to the idea of being 'daring', I still struggled to put my finger on exactly why 'dare' felt so fitting.

Then some connections arose for me. Early on in my training, Qapel said the two things that are most important for a student to progress on the Path are a heart of compassion and ruthless self-honesty. I realized that being 'daring' isn't necessarily about facing danger, but rather it's about breaking away from conventional or societal thinking. To ask questions about what is actually going on is to be daring. It's an invitation to step into a new way of knowing and being. By being truly curious and willing to look at what might be, we are risking everything (that we know). In the end, the daring part is to see what's beyond, what's actually possible.

The content of the following pages will range from entertaining, intriguing, eye-opening, or deeply transformative for you, depending on the aspiration you hold while you read it. The stories, metaphors and insights Qapel offers can act simply as inspiration, or as cut-to-the bone truths. How deeply you allow the wisdom to transform you depends on how daring you are.

For those of you who have never had the chance to be in a room with Qapel, the material in this book—drawn from transcripts of talks given during public appearances and retreats—offers the closest taste of his voice in writings to date. It embodies his greatest strengths, and points to his legacy: teachings that are practical, humorous, and deeply rooted in compassion for all beings.

Christopher Lawley
Producer of the *Dharma If You Dare* podcast

NAMO TASSA BHAGAVATO ARAHATO SAMMA SAMBUDDHASSA

SPOKEN IN THE ANCIENT PALI LANGUAGE, this traditional homage simply means, "I name this state as being a good state." In terms of the path of liberation, this assertion is highly important. Back in the time of the Buddha, around 500 B.C., there were many meditation masters, and often disciples of different ones would meet on the road and ask each other what their teachers taught. One day, two women met and one asked the other, "What can your teacher do?" "Well, he can change the weather and he can even walk on the clouds!" "Very good." The other woman asked in turn, "Who is your teacher?" "My teacher is The Buddha." she replied. "And what can he do?" "Well, he knows the wholesome for the wholesome and the unwholesome for the unwholesome."

Now that's not going to sell many movies. I mean, what would you rather get—the big wow or the recognition of the wholesome for the wholesome and the unwholesome for the unwholesome? I think most people in this generation are going to go for the wow. But, in fact, the path of liberation is walked and realized on the basis of small moments of understanding.

On his deathbed, the Buddha said, "Pay attention to detail." Where freedom actually lies for us is in the details, and the liberation moment occurs when we fall in the gap between two details.

Enjoy the journey!

Qapel Doug Duncan

CHAPTER

1

BEAUTIFULLY BENT TREES AND THE FOREST OF EMPTINESS:
Rediscovering your true nature

ONE OF MY MOST POWERFUL CHILDHOOD MEMORIES is when my family moved from our old house with a leaky roof and corners that didn't quite meet to a brand new house in suburbia. The message blinking across my mother's forehead was, "We made it!" I was about six years old at the time. One day as she was unpacking boxes, I found my crayons and started drawing on her new walls with purple, red, and blue. I was ecstatic! But when she came in and saw my work of art, all hell broke loose. The experience taught me that it's wrong to draw on walls, and more significantly, that bliss can be interrupted. Gradually, I learned to downplay bliss because I experienced over and over again that events which brought me great joy never lasted.

As a child, to accommodate the wishes of your two all-powerful parental figures, you bent and molded yourself, like a tree grows around a rock or a fence post. The interruptions of one parent twisted your tree trunk one way, while those of the other parent twisted it in another. Siblings, relatives, and friends had some impact, but by and large it was your mom and dad. Because this shaping happened so early in life, it's largely unconscious.

You see this conditioning in other people as their idiosyncrasies. People seem odd to you because you believe that your trunk is straight. You think to yourself, "I know I have my problems, but basically I'm together. But this *other* person is very, very strange. I don't understand how their trunk got *so bent!*" Of course, bent trees are perfectly good; they still bear fruit. This is, in fact, what the enlightened mind sees—beautifully bent trees!

Meditation helps you become aware of how early childhood experiences influence your choices, opinions, and feelings. One meaning of the word "persona" is mask. Your personality is made up of the masks you use to relate to the world. When you embark on a spiritual journey, you begin to shift your attention away from making your masks work for you to understanding how they were formed. You begin to ask questions, such as, "Do my masks serve a purpose?" "Can I change them?" "Do I even want to use them?"

When something upsets you, often it is because you're not getting what you want or you're getting what you don't want. Your automatic reaction is to point a finger—"It's his fault!" This is the persona's number one defense against knowing how it was built. If you can blame the other person, then you don't have to see your part in the problem. Why does the persona do this? Because, if it admits that it was also at fault, then it has to recognize that it's not perfect. A defective persona implies, "I'm not perfect." This conclusion puts one at risk of abandonment and rejection. Thus the persona has a huge vested interest in not knowing about its masquerade and will do whatever it takes to avoid admitting its flaws.

The Room At The End Of The Hall

My teacher used to say that Dharma is the room at the end of the hall, the one you will enter only after having exhausted all other possibilities for finding happiness and relief from suffering. The path to this room is to study the patterns of our childhood, our family and tribal conditioning, to see how our ego structure was built. Such exploration requires strong focus. All spiritual practices, no matter what religion, are basically to provide the strength and courage to keep from getting distracted by the loud voices of the persona as one attempts to penetrate it.

On this journey we discover that all suffering stems from our likes and dislikes—chasing after the pleasant and avoiding the unpleasant. Our proclivities are based on conditioning; they're a result of our personal mapping system—how we relate to others and our surroundings through our senses, thoughts, and speech.

The transcendental consciousness, on the other hand, is based on pure, unbiased perception. For example, say you're having a discussion with your friend and you both stop talking. Your dominant awareness is probably visual if she's in front of you. But when she starts talking again, your awareness becomes more auditory. If she triggers ideas, your awareness becomes more conceptual. If she hits a sensitive spot in your conditioning, then your awareness becomes more emotional. This is how the awakened mind works—it simply records what is occurring in the moment without judgment.

If you begin to observe yourself in relation to others and the material world, you'll see that it's very hard to act outside the box of your conditioning. Though you have the ability to do so, it's going to cost you your identity. Suffering doesn't stem from how you were conditioned, but from clinging to your knowledge, feelings, ideas, and most significantly, your body.

With awakening you don't lose your individuality. Instead, your reference point becomes the totality of the forest, not your single, little sapling. Being fully aware in this moment without wanting or pushing away any object that appears in consciousness is *sunyata*, "emptiness or unlimited potential." In particular, this is horrifying to the ego because it's so fully identified with being this tree. But the fact is that you could have been any tree in the forest.

Bliss Interruptus

The meditative journey takes you back to the earliest upset in your consciousness—when you realized that you and your mother were separate people. This happened when your feelings of blissful union were interrupted. For instance, one day you were lying in your crib staring at a mobile. Babies can do this for hours at a time, completely absorbed in the object. But your mother, fearing that you were going into a coma, picked you up. This is a natural maternal response, but the distraction caused a twist in your trunk. Over time you began to develop the idea that the function of your mother was to interrupt your bliss.

Another time you were happily gazing at the mobile and reached out for it. Not being able to grasp it, you started to cry. If your mother came in and gave it to you, you learned that by crying you'd be satisfied—another twist in your trunk. Or, if she didn't, you learned that crying wouldn't do any good, so you stopped.

As you continued to develop, you started to interrupt your own bliss because preempting mother gave you a feeling of control, however false, in an otherwise chaotic world. This tendency to disturb your own peace is what you begin to see when you sit on the meditation cushion.

This is not to blame parents. They were only trying to teach you behavior that was socially acceptable and safe. Yet interruptions dominate the socialization process—"Eat your spinach! Brush your teeth! Don't play with matches!"

Abandonment is the flip side of the coin. Mother was busy doing laundry, so you didn't have her attention and felt rejected. The ego structure then develops in response to that terrifying feeling of being left alone. Another twist in the trunk.

Meditation allows you to see that whenever you are interrupted or challenged, you react like a two-year-old—pouting or throwing a tantrum. You may not show that behavior to anyone except your intimate partner or family, but this is what's going on inside you. Seeing through your conditioning will allow you to choose your response rather than operate from a knee-jerk reaction to parental authority.

To illustrate this point, let's say my father Harry is overbearing and my habitual, conditioned reaction is to fight against him. So whenever I'm around anybody who reminds me of him I become angry and confrontational. An awakened being, however, doesn't react in this way. No matter how domineering Harry is behaving, a clear consciousness sees his suffering and generates loving-kindness and compassion for him.

Q: *Are you saying that conditioning doesn't exist for awakened beings?*

Conditioning has been transcended. This doesn't change the fact that my father is domineering or that as a pre-awakened consciousness I fought against him. But as an awakened consciousness, it's not necessary to maintain that pattern because I know that my reaction to this kind of behavior is how I was conditioned. Now I am free to respond in any number of ways, from saying, "Okay Harry, if that's the way you want it, then fine, go ahead," or standing up to him and saying, "Hey look Harry, that's causing suffering. Please stop."

Only those who themselves are suffering cause pain to others. Because you no longer associate other people's pain as being your problem, you're not controlled by it. Therefore, you have no motivation to hurt others. In a sense, your ego has died to the situation.

Whenever your conditioned mind isn't there, you experience bliss. However, the moment you start dialoguing with whatever is arising in consciousness, the bliss diminishes. For instance, say you're looking at a sunset and are experiencing bliss. It would be great if you could just rest in that state, but sooner or later the voices of the persona return. They say, "Oh, I want the sunset to last," or, "I wish my partner could see this," or, "The only reason the sunset is beautiful is because of the pollution." The ego is very skillful in finding ways to interrupt you from the pure feeling of bliss itself. So why do you interrupt bliss? Because you *want* to be interrupted; it keeps *you* there.

To see through the ego's disruptive patterns, you need a refuge. That refuge is the mind that can be free from obsessive self-referencing. Try opening up to the *possibility* of emptiness, even if you don't see it yet. Then start observing the mind and become aware of its contours. The next time you feel threatened, see how your patterning determines your reaction. You have to learn how to transcend the interruptions without resisting them, how to go in and out of bliss, *regardless of circumstances*. No matter how badly you are treated, you must be able to access joy with a snap of your fingers.

In your investigation of phenomena you will start to notice a very simple process: out of nowhere everything arises, lasts for a time, and passes away. Take anger, for example. Is anger lasting and permanent? Doesn't it pass away? The same is true of desire—it arises, lasts for a time, and then disappears.

Q: *How do I move through anger? Is it being able to step outside of myself and watch the anger come and go?*

Let's take it step-by-step. First, you're often not aware of anger until you're already angry, and then you deny it. You think to yourself, "I'm *not* angry. Maybe I'm being a bit forceful, but I'm not angry." You convince yourself that the other person deserves what you're dishing out. This is how human beings generally operate.

Next you think, "Okay, *maybe* this is anger, but I know what I'm doing. I'm being angry intentionally." Then you say to yourself, "All right, this is anger. I shouldn't be feeling this because I'm a holy person." And although you pretend you're not angry, the fact is you still are.

The following stage is, "I know I'm angry and I'm acting as if I'm not, so I've got to change this by being loving." Then you start faking it—"Oh yes, I love you." It's like some horror movie where the monster tries to keep its face together while it's obviously falling apart. This is the shadow aspect of your being.

Eventually, you realize that the only way to defeat anger is to leave it alone—allow it to be there but not identify with it. This takes time because of the subtle tricks you use to deal with heated situations, but eventually, with practice, you can do it. You start to see anger's triggering mechanism before you actually get angry. You see the wave coming and say, "Oh, anger is arising." And you watch it build. You think, "This is interesting. How long is this state of anger going to last?" Gradually, it starts to subside. You have more freedom now because you can see the wave before it takes you under.

As you learn to witness intense emotions you begin to understand that you can have the same intensity of energy without the emotion. Now you can look angry but not actually *be* angry; this is wrathful compassion. The energy is still present, but since it is no longer associated with your personal reaction, you remain clear. This energy can now be used to benefit someone else. It has the power to cut through ignorance and interrupt unwholesome habits.

Q: *If you see anger coming and say, "That's interesting. I'm getting angry," does that mean you won't actually get angry?*

If you don't get caught when someone says, "You're stupid!" then you're safe. But it doesn't take much for you to blow up, does it? When you catch yourself and say, "Okay, hold it, my button got pushed," you are acknowledging that you're angry and can then examine what sensations arise in the body. As you do, the anger gradually dissolves. When you're at that point then, in a sense, you're no longer there. Whatever anybody does to you, whatever anybody says to you, however anybody treats you—either nicely or badly, praising or blaming you, it's just wind blowing through an empty room.

Becoming A Scientist

To transcend the ego you have to scrutinize it very closely. You must observe it like an entomologist would an ant or a physicist would neutrinos until you see that essentially all of your actions are motivated by egoistic self-involvement. When you become completely aware of this, you will get a glimpse of the clear radiant state. Trust is allowing yourself to see how unrelenting the preoccupation with self is.

Your whole being becomes the laboratory, the artist's studio, the theater. When you gain insight into your own reactive patterns, you begin to have greater compassion for others' negative behavior. Gradually, this wisdom becomes more and more evident, and hatred, lust, and confusion begin to wane. When you understand that the universe is doing nothing but having a huge party—including suffering, decay and death—and that only your conditioning makes life painful, then liberation is close at hand.

For more resources on the topic of spiritual refuge,
visit planetdharma.com/dare/resources.

Quick investment, quick return

CHAPTER

2

ABSORPTION 101:
Befriending the meditation cushion

Developing the ability to go into full meditative absorption in three breaths is only slightly more complicated than putting your clothes on in the morning. Anyone can do it; you're just not used to focusing your mind. Instead, you have become conditioned to respond to constant change. The catchphrase in your day-to-day life is "quick investment, quick return."

Regardless of the challenges of living in such fast-paced times, you must meditate in order to understand that what goes on in your world is perfectly fine just as it is. To lead a life of bliss and clarity, this discipline is not an option; it's a necessity. Meditation itself is not the reward, but the accompanying joy, freedom, and wisdom are.

Absorption happens whenever you are completely engaged in what you're doing. So, if you're taking out the garbage, cleaning the bathroom, or even riding your bike through crowded city streets and you're fully focused on the task, you're meditating. Active meditations such as these are great, but they can't take you into more fully absorbed states of consciousness that sitting in formal meditation can.

People who practice regularly can describe their meditations in detail. They might talk about physical sensations, recurring thoughts, maybe even mention an insight or two. If you have never meditated, though, you might not notice anything happening at all. Actually, it's impossible for *nothing* to happen. If you had nothing happen for a whole hour you would probably be considered a Buddha. In that hour all sorts of things happened—you got restless, your knees hurt, you wondered what's on TV, and you asked yourself if meditation was worth your time. You thought about your work and your relationships. You even had moments of calm and clarity. But it's all too easy to miss those moments because you're conditioned to react to a constant stream of phenomena.

With practice, meditation can open you up to subtle levels of awareness. The depth of your experience will be determined by your aspiration. But first you need to get beyond your resistance, behind the voice that says, "I can't focus long enough on this" or, "I don't want to spend all of my time here." These self-defeating thoughts send you back to the shopping mall or your computer screen. You must make a strong commitment to sit still long enough to go through the distracting machinations of the mind.

The reason your life has developed to the degree it has thus far is because somewhere along the line you made the effort to know something you didn't know, or to do something you never tried before. That exploration took you beyond your previous level of understanding. Most people, however, spend their time milling about in a world they already know.

The realms you explore in meditation don't require "you." It's like playing a musical instrument with full concentration. The *"you"*—the ego—drops away. You still know what you're doing, but you recognize that the ego is not important to the process. This is the beginning of meditative absorption. You don't disappear, as if somebody took an eraser and wiped your name off the chalkboard. It is not a negation of you, but rather a kind of forgetting of you. In this state, time and space fall away. It might last for an hour or a day. Most people can remain there about twenty minutes, ten minutes if they're preoccupied, or five if they're restless. When someone doesn't value the state at all, absorption will last a mere second and be gone.

A Burning House

Surprisingly, the more you practice meditation and forget about you, the more control you actually gain. Even though meditation involves giving up control, it results in giving you better control of your life. When a negative influence comes along and smacks you on the head, you don't get caught. Wise instincts tell you to flee from negative states as you would a burning house—throw your valuables out the window, get out, and call the fire department. You don't panic because you know it won't help. You've observed negative states over and over again in meditation and realize that being hateful, greedy, or critical is not going to get you where you want to go.

Bringing one's mind back to the positive can be done in myriad ways—by playing the flute, working in the garden, even learning to tango! Formal meditation has two vehicles: *samatha* and *vipassana*. *Samatha* is the development of calm and concentration, which leads to bliss. Chanting, visualization, *mudra* (movement), and devotional meditations are all types of *samatha* meditation. *Vipassana*, or "insight meditation," is an analytical approach leading to wisdom and understanding by connecting ideas. These two aspects, the dry insight and the more emotional bliss, go hand in hand.

Liberation through the path of insight *can* be easier than the path of bliss because the mind is not so greedy for stimulation. Intellectual people are drawn to it because their minds can keep tossing ideas around—something they're used to doing. In general, though, they tend not to go into bliss because they don't allow themselves to let go of the internal dialogue long enough to see what happens. They're afraid that if they lose it, they'll lose their identity, so they always keep it present as an umbilical cord back to "normalcy." The key is simply letting go.

Insight can also be harder because you fall in love with your own mind—"Oh, that was such a smart thought! Yes! But I have a comment on that…Oh, oh! Even more brilliant!" Or you have these meditative experiences of vast space and infinite consciousness and you brag—"Yes, well, I experienced pure love the other day. No big deal." There's nothing worse than pride. Plugging into "the source" does not give you license to claim special status. It's everyone's birthright—the mark of being human. Everyone is born with the capacity for the awakened state.

Is Meditation Necessary?

Some people are afraid they might go crazy from meditating. But, in a way, you already are. There are three levels of the brain which all have different impulses: the instinctual brain says, "Eat, procreate, stay warm, and survive;" the emotional brain says, "Have fun, meet your friends, find a relationship;" the mental brain says, "Go here, do this, retire, move, and buy." The brain also has two hemispheres: the left analytical sphere and the right creative one; so you can see, you're already a divided house.

When you start to meditate you are mediating between all these disparate parts. It can get noisy inside your head because you have never really listened to all the different parts and each has something to say. You might get exasperated and say, "Just let me watch a movie!" But if you have the aspiration to see what happens once these parts start to settle, you'll notice that they begin to merge. When this happens, you become calmer. The more calm and focused you are, the more energetic you feel. It's a formula: put in two parts concentration, one part aspiration, stir with time, and let it rise. Joy happens automatically.

Your *effort* is what brings the bliss. This is the number one lesson in life: what brings joy is not getting the object. It comes from making a conscious effort to participate in the process. If there's no effort, there's no joy. A trust fund baby doesn't feel joy by getting a lot of money. If, on the other hand, you've had to work hard to earn a livelihood, you're so much richer for having made the effort. The examples are endless—working on a mathematical problem, learning how to do a triple axel in skating, mastering a foreign language, etc. In all of these situations, having a strong intention to engage in the process, regardless of the outcome, is what creates the bliss.

The same joy arises through bringing your mind back again and again while learning to meditate. This process leads to a greater sense of compassion for others' struggles. In meditation you come to know yourself, and in doing that you know everybody. If you realize how your own frustration and irritation arise, you have greater understanding toward other people's negative mind states. When you become aware of your own fear or uncertainty, you can appreciate those same feelings in others. This understanding automatically generates compassion rather than criticism. It is only when you deny your failings that you criticize others for reflecting them back to you.

We ignore our weaknesses because we're afraid we'll be deemed unlovable if we own up to them. In fact, this fear is an irrational projection of the mind. If you go right to the core of the feeling, stay there, and look clearly at the fear in your being, you'll find that it dissolves, no matter how much you expect it not to. The problem is that you just don't stay at the core long enough; you veer off before the fear has a chance to be released. If you hang in there, fear will vanish on its own.

By shifting your view from "This is weird" or "This is scary" to "This is interesting," any negative emotion will fall away. Keep in mind we're talking about meditating—not about driving down the highway with your eyes closed or jumping off a high building without a parachute. The practice is to sit still or walk mindfully to explore how consciousness works.

Perseverance will enrich you in your day-to-day life. The awareness gained through meditation will be there when you go shopping or meet your friend for lunch. Any experience will become fuller and deeper because you'll be more focused and present.

Meditation as a study of consciousness is much more interesting than whether I like something or not or whether I'm happy or not. It's much more interesting than whether anybody likes me or not. The eight worldly concerns—praise/blame, fame/shame, pleasure/pain, loss/gain—gradually fall away. They still arise, but they no longer hold your attention because they're not nearly as interesting as the study of how consciousness works.

If somebody calls you a jerk, the only reason you suffer is because you're attached to an identity. But if you instead focus on how consciousness operates, then being called a jerk becomes interesting only in terms of its biochemical effect on the body. Gradually, our opinions and feelings begin to have less and less power over us. They're still there, but they no longer elicit a knee-jerk reaction.

Letting go of past hurts is crucial. You might claim, "Oh, I was hurt! This happened to me!" Yes, but you're not there now; you're here. Or you might think, "I've got to resolve this." In fact, you don't! You will never resolve anything that has already happened. You must acknowledge it, but then walk on. If you put your energy into retribution, you end up becoming the thing you hate. Your ego will be obsessed with whether you're getting the respect or reward you think you deserve. This is very human, but it won't take you into bliss. In fact, it keeps you away from bliss, locked in repetitive patterns. What's the point of that when you could be in a state of joy?

Meditation Is Your Choice

Deciding to meditate isn't your teacher's choice. It is your choice. You decide at any given moment whether or not you're going to be in a clear, radiant state. The only thing that truly benefits society is people who are in states of bliss and clarity. It's better to be clear and do *nothing* than to do amazing things motivated by greed or hatred. When you're in a clear state, almost anything you do makes people happy.

To achieve clarity, I recommend that you set aside some time for meditation each day, stay actively engaged in your life, and trust that things will unfold in a natural way. If you take this attitude, recognizing that you're exactly where you're supposed to be, doing exactly what you're supposed to be doing, you'll die happy and fulfilled; it will have been a successful life. If you don't, you'll die with regrets about things you didn't do and people you didn't love.

So, move inch by inch. Start with something you're currently interested in and let it extend out from there. For example, say you're interested in motorcycles—in how they work and how to fix them. Then you expand your interest to racing motorcycles competitively. Or, you start riding motorcycles in the circus. Then you get interested in trapezes, and later, in how they are made, so you go back to school and become an engineer.

When you allow your interest to unfold, you'll find that the problem is no longer that you're tired, but that you don't have enough time to pursue it. Instead of saying, "I'm exhausted, I have to go to bed—life is so hard," you'll say, "Give me more hours in the day."

Try to see past the negative self-talk—"Oh, I'm not good at that," or "I can't do it right," and just throw yourself into the process. It's not the activity that's important, but the state of mind that you bring to it. In a monastery you're taught that if you're going to sweep the floor, just sweep the floor. If you're going to do the dishes, just do the dishes—don't listen to the radio or look over your shoulder to see who's there. Gradually, the training will pervade everything you do.

A positive state of mind will give you greater courage. Then, when you decide to make a change, you won't hesitate. You might examine an opportunity from different points of view, but you won't be paralyzed by telling yourself, "I can't do this. What will other people think?!" Who cares if you look like a fool? You're stepping out of the box! Being impolite or breaking the rules is not the goal, but your explorations may take you past the point where other people think you should go. Often it's simply what we *imagine* other people will think of us that holds us back.

The bottom line is that to live a fuller life, you have to be willing to go deeper into absorption and be more committed in your involvements. The more you trust and throw yourself into the experience, the more your confidence will grow. The joy that results from living with abandon will more than compensate for whether or not people like you.

Q: *What's the best way to clear my mind when I try to meditate?*

Don't try to clear your mind—that's a recipe for failure. First of all, keep your back straight. If you're sitting in a chair, bring your back away from it so that the energies in your body can realign. Second, don't try to do anything. Find an interesting object and throw yourself into it. So if you like flowers, put a few white roses in a bowl of water, and just jump in. Whatever comes up, say, "White roses, white roses." That's your mantra. The minute you start looking around, repeat, "White roses, white roses."

The point is not to hypnotize yourself but to quiet your habitual chatter. When your mind says, "This is stupid" and "I'm wasting my time," continue to say, "Okay, white roses, white roses, white roses." Allow your mind to settle. Whenever it wanders off, bring it back without criticism, like a parent lovingly spoon-feeding applesauce to an infant.

Start with short sessions—perhaps ten minutes, two times a day. You can change the meditation object, but recognize that what's more interesting than the object itself is the tendency for your attention to drift—"Why all of a sudden am I bored with these roses? I wasn't bored with them five minutes ago." You're not trying to measure how successfully you focus your mind on the object but simply watching how consciousness tries to move you all over the room. Just acknowledge it. Don't get upset or frustrated. Don't think, "I failed," or "I can't do this."

Anything can happen when you do become fully absorbed in the roses. If you suddenly find yourself in a field of white roses that transforms into an infinite cloud bank of dancing goddesses scattering flowers on your head, don't panic. Just say, "Yeah, that's interesting. White roses, white roses." Don't let the amazing things that happen— the great states of excitement, tears flowing, feeling as if some god has just come down and made you his or her consort—distract you.

Don't go up and don't go down; just keep thinking, "White roses, white roses...." Up will come—you will experience states you never dreamed were possible in human consciousness. And then down will come, and you'll think, "I'm going crazy! I'm going crazy!" But then simply say to yourself, "Yeah, yeah! Shut up! White roses...."

The Freedom Of A Focused Consciousness

Blissful clarity is your birthright as a human being. The capacity to focus your consciousness and enter states of bliss is what enables you to act compassionately.

But ordinarily you get trapped in knee-jerk reactions. In order to free yourself from unwholesome patterns, train yourself to shift your consciousness with intention. What takes you into unpleasant states is the habitual tendency not to meditate. What brings clarity is meditation, and with practice, it becomes very easy. Even unwholesome states are interesting in their own way—"Why do I always feel criticized? Why does this person get under my skin?" If you see this kind of investigation as a job, you won't want to do it. You do this work because you are going to awaken. You cannot imagine the freedom and joy that will come into your life when you do it. It's what Jesus promised, what Buddha promised. The path to awakening has always been there, but you have to choose it. For the ego it's work, but for the awakened mind it is infinite play.

For more resources on various meditation practices,
visit planetdharma.com/dare/resources.

CHAPTER

3

600 TUBES OF TOOTHPASTE:
Creativity and karma

CHUCK YEAGER, THE TEST PILOT famous for breaking many speed and altitude records, basically set the tone on facing adversity for all airline pilots with his nonchalant, cowboy attitude. Now, male pilots in the aviation industry copy his style— "Hello. This is Dan Smith, your captain speaking. We're flying at 30,000 feet over Tennessee. It's pretty rough out, with hurricanes and lightning storms, but we'll do our best to give you a comfortable ride." Emulating Yeager is an effective way for pilots to stay cool under pressure. It's a good recipe, but there's no freedom in it. If you want to stretch yourself beyond the limits imposed by society, you need to break the mold and develop your imagination.

Most people lock themselves into habitual patterns that block creativity. These patterns become obvious when you meditate. If you observe what grabs the mind, you will notice that it follows well-worn paths: to your job if you work a lot, to your children if you're a parent. Your emotions follow your thoughts and will be positive or negative depending on how well you like your job or how your relationship is going. Your body follows your emotions. Simply stated, your meditation will be a reflection of your life.

Karma, which means "action," is to travel on familiar roads, allowing you only familiar experiences. When I was in the third grade and drew pictures with blue trees, my teacher told me, "Trees are not blue, they're green." Primarily, children are trained to be useful to society, which in itself is not a bad thing. However, insofar as society has a limited range of ideas about usefulness, you develop a limited range of creativity. To change your karma, you have to make a conscious decision to change your behavior. It's not going to work if you tell yourself you're going to be a spiritual being but wind up spending most of your time stuck in the same old habits.

The first step to unleashing your creative potential is to become aware of the mind's ruts. Your karma is to cling to the past as if it were happening now. But no matter how dreadful your past was, it's the past. It's unlikely that in your meditation session someone will jump through the roof and attack you, or your high school sweetheart will call and chastise you for eloping with the cheerleader. You are probably in a safe, contained environment, so you have no reason to be afraid. Most likely, your only concern is what might happen in your own mind. As Mahatma Gandhi said, "The only devils in this world are those running around in our own hearts, and that is where all our battles should be fought."

This moment is all there is. Fully experiencing it, no laws exist except those of the body: the heart pumps blood, the lungs take in and expel air, digestion takes place. Yet your emotional and mental patterns remain fixed in place unless you make a conscious effort to break out of them.

Practicing meditation calls into question all the thoughts, beliefs, judgments, etc., that run through your mind. These partial views, imposed on you by family, church, school, and others (mostly with good intention), have stifled your imagination. Once you no longer see this conditioning as a solid "you," you open up to a greater range of opportunity. Your explorations will give you the courage to resist the tendency to move toward safety and comfort, especially as you age.

Roasted Crickets Anyone?

If you want to grow, take the quick path to liberation by undertaking challenges. Then watch the body, feelings, and states of mind. Challenges send a message to the depth of your being that you want a more expansive life. The spiritual life begins and ends with discovery, becoming aware. To discover, you must extend your limits. So, once a week do something a little difficult, once a month do something more difficult, and once a year try something that seems impossible.

The once-a-week challenge is training wheels—doing something just a little bit out of the ordinary. Go jogging, or turn off your computer for a day, just to see if you can do it. If it's hard for you not to buy anything for a day, that's a weekly challenge.

The once-a-month challenge is like riding a bicycle with no hands—something you wouldn't normally do unless you set your mind to it. Speaking in public, cooking a meal for someone, and changing the oil in your car are a few examples. Self-esteem and self-confidence issues will surface with the bigger challenges. However, the trepidation is almost always much greater than the event itself.

As a monthly challenge, two Dharma students ate roasted crickets in Burma. Shine, our Burmese guide, smiled—"Oh, crickets. Great!" Only a lack of imagination prevents crickets from joining potato chips and pretzels on your list of munchies. Such minor decisions don't seem to make much difference, but in fact they do, because if you can't be imaginative in your choice of a snack, how will you be imaginative in your choice of a career?

After you have built up some confidence by doing weekly and monthly challenges, you're ready for the big one! The once-a-year challenge is free-falling through empty space; it's over the edge and seemingly impossible because it forces you to directly confront your sense of identity. Perhaps this challenge is something you've avoided your entire life. Keep it relatively wholesome and non-life-threatening, such as learning how to scuba dive or traveling alone to a foreign country.

Q: *I've read that to be creative you should put your books away, but I've never wanted to do that.*

Growth and liberation come in two ways: either by doing what you wanted to do but were afraid to, or by doing what you thought you ought to do but found reasons not to. In either case the important thing is to break through preconceived views of self. The particular action doesn't matter. You needn't give up reading forever. But because the mind looks for something to occupy itself with, not reading for a weekend would allow you to turn inward and experience something new.

Liberation Begins In The Body

Liberation occurs first and foremost in the body. When undertaking a challenge, you must acknowledge the body's response to fear and make your peace with it. It is natural for some shaking and quaking to occur when on the edge of a new experience. Rather than panicking and trying to escape, track the experience like a scientist—"Heart rate is up...face is flushed…breathing is shallow and quick." Simply acknowledge what is taking place and the body relaxes.

Do your challenges and then take it easy the rest of the time. If you're somebody who gets caught up in endless self-improvement, the challenges are an alternative to constantly agonizing over the need to change yourself. Worrying gets you nowhere; it actually exhausts the energy you need to do something new.

Breaking Karmic Chains

If you are not in a clear, radiant state moment to moment, then you lack imagination, not ability or intelligence. There is no reason why you can't be in a state of bliss all day long. And if you trained yourself to be clear throughout your day, it would start making your sleeping hours radiant too.

Life offers plenty of opportunities to be imaginative, but few people accept them. Most are limited by the parameters they've set for themselves that are like stakes in the ground—"This is as far as I go. I won't move beyond this point." The litany of reasons goes something like this: "I've been hurt before. I can't afford it. What will happen when I get old? I'm tired. I have a busy day tomorrow. My mother will find out." These are the karmic chains that keep our hearts locked in.

Q: *It all seems to be based on the fear of loss. No Friday night pizza would mean losing the comfort it provides.*

Absolutely. Fear of loss is central. Look at your relationships. You might think, "I can't tell her what I actually think because she won't love me anymore." Or "I can't do that—my friends would make fun of me." The fact is, however, that you never lose anything by exercising your imagination; you only gain.

Ironically, fear of loss tends to actually produce loss. When you're afraid, you draw in an inch. Six months later you fear losing something else, so you draw in another inch. This is why you tend to get more rigid as you grow older. When you were twenty, you would try anything. Now you have a job to keep, things to look after, and are afraid that life won't support you, so you become less flexible.

The vast majority of your fears are unfounded. People who have suffered traumatic accidents often say, "It sounds weird but it's the best thing that ever happened to me. I've learned to be a completely different person." Lose your legs and you discover how precious it is to have hands; lose your innocence and you gain maturity. Overcoming the fear of loss of power and control is crucial to keep you from growing increasingly bitter with age.

Replacing Fear With Curiosity

The Tibetans face the fear of loss directly by creating sand mandalas—painstakingly intricate masterpieces that represent the entire universe. Five or six monks spend twenty hours a day for a week building them. Then the mandalas are swept away in a two-hour ceremony.

Like these monks, you must train yourself to not be limited by the fear of pain or loss. Use difficult experiences to make yourself wiser and more compassionate; there is no other purpose in life. Besides, no matter how hard you try to get comfortable, you won't succeed because age is creeping up on you. Eventually, you'll be on your deathbed and nothing will save you. Learn to accept loss now so that when death comes you can say, "Hmm…let's see what's over there."

Q: *Can't a routine serve as a tool for liberation? Having pizza every Friday night may free you from worrying about what to eat, so you can explore in other ways.*

It is true, as the saying goes: "The greatest freedom lies within the strongest discipline." But you need to ask yourself the purpose of your routine. Is it to keep you undisturbed? You have to be honest with yourself. It may be that you don't want to face something.

Changing The Dance

A partnership or marriage is one place where you can't hide; your habitual tendencies are laid out in the open. It's an excellent training ground for developing patience and flexibility. The day-to-day stuff is what trips you up—your partner's dramatic flair which you used to love now really irritates you. Big things you somehow find the spirit to forgive and forget; it's the little things that can take the love out of a marriage.

Q: *My husband always leaves the cap off the toothpaste. Should I confront him or do I have to accept that for the rest of my life that's the way it's going to be?*

There are other options. Take the entire tube of toothpaste and squeeze it all over his brush. Now it's his turn to be upset. Or buy 600 tubes of toothpaste and bring out a new tube whenever he leaves the cap off. This action may not get him to replace the cap, but it will free *your* mind from being locked into a particular pattern by his habit. The reason you're bothered is because your habits conflict. That's the entire point—your life is habitual!

You could make it a game. Flirt! "If you put the cap back on ... well ... we could ... mmmm ..." Why not? Make it fun. Try to be more adaptable in your approach to things. It could change the entire dialogue from "my will versus your will," where all conflict starts, to, "How can my will and your will dance without getting angry, bitter, and frustrated?" Change the dance. Do the bunny hop or the hokey-pokey instead of the waltz. Use your imagination! This is how you change your karma.

Here arises one very telling and uncomfortable point: you don't want to change your karma. You hope that your life will change without actually having to do anything about it. If you live with another human being there will always be a conflict of wills. How you face that contest determines how well you will function with other people in the world. You need to move past your position and see the issue within the context of compassion and loving-kindness. Remember that you are what you hate while you hate it; this is a very important lesson. In the moment that you hate the person who is abusing you, you are the abuser. The lesson to be learned is to love the other person even if you don't approve of his or her behavior.

Don't stay stuck in your patterns. Isn't this the rule of relationship? If you're inflexible, the other person will be equally inflexible. If, with good intent, you become more agreeable, he or she is likely to become more agreeable too.

Little Movies In Your Head

The key battle is not the struggle between you and your partner, but rather what's going on *inside* you. Remember, the small things keep you stuck. Meditation takes you to the place where your yardsticks constantly shift. One day the angels are singing and you're smiling

"En garde!"

like an Indian guru. The next day it's, "I'm such a loser." As different states of mind arise, you realize that none of them are you; they're just little movies playing in your head. When you realize this, you can say what the Dalai Lama said when someone asked him who he was: "I'm anything you want me to be…plus *sunyata* (emptiness or unlimited potential)." That's where freedom lies. Freedom says I can be anything I want to be—from professor to poet to macho man to dance hall girl. If you have the ability to *become* the other person rather than only be in *relationship* to them, the boundaries disappear.

Milarepa And The Seven Demons

"The Song of Perfect Assurance (to the Demons)," sacred poetry written by the great yogi Milarepa, is about embracing your fears. Milarepa became an orphan at a young age and lost all of his family's belongings to greedy relatives. Seeking revenge, he learned black magic and used it to murder thirty-five of his relatives. Later he came to regret terribly what he had done. To make amends he retreated to a cave to meditate. One day, he went outside to collect firewood. When he came back, he found seven demons of his past in the cave. They were gigantic and had saucer-like eyes. Milarepa was frightened and repeated a mantra to calm himself. Still, the demons remained. He decided that anything so awesome must have something to teach him, so he sang them a song of friendship:

> *You demons gathered here are obstacles.*
> *Drink this nectar of friendliness and compassion.*

Three of the seven demons who had been playing tricks on him faded away. Milarepa gained strength and determined that the four demons which were left were magical obstacles, so he sang them a song of confidence:

> *It is wonderful that you demons came today.*
> *You must come again tomorrow.*
> *From time to time we should talk together.*

When they heard this, three of the four demons turned into rainbows and disappeared.

The last demon did a horrifying dance and Milarepa thought, "This one is powerful and vicious." So he sang it a song of surrender:

> *If a demon like you could intimidate me*
> *Compassion would have little meaning.*
> *Demon, if you stay longer, that is fine with me.*
> *If you have friends, bring them along.*
> *If we have differences, we will talk them out.*

Afterwards, filled with compassion, Milarepa climbed into the demon's mouth and it vanished.

If you step into the middle of fear, and allow it to envelop you, it will dissolve. It's like being in the eye of the hurricane. If you want freedom, increase your range. Use your imagination and do something new—whatever challenges you. Lighten up! Don't take yourself so seriously. Have some fun. Life's supposed to be fun—suffering, yes, but fun suffering.

For more resources on the topic of undertaking challenges, visit planetdharma.com/dare/resources.

CHAPTER

4

BIG ROCKS:
Discovering your purpose

IMAGINE IF YOU PUT A FEW BIG ROCKS in a bathtub, then filled in the rest with sand. If somebody looked at it, they would probably assume that it was only sand because that's all they would see. The same is true for our lives. If we don't get beneath the sand, the incessant demands of life will overwhelm us and we'll forget our true purpose for being here.

What are your big rocks? What's your reason for living other than to just get through the week? Most of your day-to-day life is spent working, shopping, cooking. Of course these activities are necessary, but are they the most important things in your life?

The big rocks represent your daemon. Daemon is akin to the word *deva*, which means "radiant" or "shining"; it's who you are called to be. What kind of person do you want to be when you're eighty-five years old, sitting in a rocking chair in an old age home? The person who finds his or her daemon is interesting to everybody, regardless of age. This person may not speak your language or have the same interests, but what you recognize in them is a person who has lived life fully rather than just gotten old and bitter.

Your calling might be to be a mother or a mechanic, an artist or an engineer. It isn't some fantasy, like becoming the next Hollywood movie star. What's important is that it moves you to embrace life completely. Still, it isn't always easy to follow your daemon. It insists that you move beyond your partial views based on race, nationality, economic class, gender, etc. Thus, from society's point of view, it's a destabilizing demon. This "demon" demands honesty and integrity and sometimes self-sacrifice.

Digging Down Deep

How do you discover your big rocks? One way is to ask yourself what you would do for free. What would you do if nobody ever rewarded you or acknowledged you for it again? In my case, I would teach Dharma whether I received any money or not because it's what I love to do. Another way is to become silent, which is the purpose for doing retreats—no reading, no TV, no socializing. The quieter you become, the easier it is for the small, knowing voice inside yourself to emerge.

The reason you don't hear your calling is because your big rocks are buried under tons of sand. Your parents helped bury your rocks; their job was to teach you to take a bath, brush your teeth, and be kind to the neighbors. Society teamed up with your parents to dump more sand on top of your rocks by preparing you to function in the world—getting an education, training, and a career.

Of course, balancing the search for the daemon with taking care of business is important. Jesus solved this dilemma by saying, "Give unto Caesar what is Caesar's." Mundane concerns are an important part of your life, but your transcendence, your unfolding as a human being, doesn't come from sand; it comes from your big rocks.

Digging down through the sand is what we do in meditation. Notice I didn't say you throw the sand out. But you must push back all your activities and create a clear, quiet, inviting space for your daemon to come forth. When you contact it, your life begins to make sense. The piles of sand, while still tedious sometimes, no longer wear you out because you're now living the life you were meant to live.

Our heroes are all people who have undertaken this quest. This is the hermit's journey—the journey of Thomas Merton and St. Teresa of Avila, Mahatma Gandhi, Rumi, Yeshe Tsogyal—people who went away from the world in order to find what they were meant to do, and then having found it, manifested it in their lives.

In the dance world, Pina Bausch and Mikhail Baryshnikov are examples of passionate, focused, committed artists following their destiny. The film *Billy Elliot* exemplifies the trials and tribulations of following your daemon. It's about a boy from a coal-mining family in northern England who wants to be a ballet dancer and has to overcome great cultural and societal pressure in order to follow his path.

We all must overcome convention to be true to ourselves. This is not to pass judgment on society and parents; they did what they were supposed to do. But you're meant for something much bigger than the tribe; you're meant for transcendence! The struggle between convention and one's higher purpose is the dialogue between the head and the heart. The head is arguing for sand—make sure you have a job, investments, a retirement plan, and the heart is saying, "Pack it up, go to Thailand, find a beach, build a life."

Your parents' fear is that if you find your daemon, you'll no longer function in society. And fair enough, there is a stage on the spiritual path when you want to retreat from the banalities of everyday life. But eventually, every good teacher pushes you back into the world in order to benefit others.

Big Rock

Taking Time Out

To identify your big rocks your mind must become quiet so that you can begin to observe yourself interacting with others. You must shift your attention from what the events are to how you experience them. For instance, instead of worrying whether or not your boss likes you, you begin to look at what in yourself cares whether or not she does. This self-observation and self-reflection creates room for your daemon to emerge.

Your new-found relationship with self will be challenging. A little voice might suddenly suggest that as a challenge to wake yourself up, you jump out of an airplane with a parachute. However, it's not going to say, "Go to Mount Kailash, shave your head, and chant 'Om' for thirty years." First, the daemon is going to test you; it's going to say, "Take up belly dancing." Of course, if you're already a belly dancer, it might say, "Take up bookkeeping" or "Learn car mechanics." By calling you to little tasks, it sees whether or not you're willing to go in a new direction. But be clear. The daemon is not some demi-god or *Lord of the Rings* creature. It's the deep understanding of what you need to do to become more genuine. The small internal movements precipitated by the challenges gradually bring you closer to this realization.

Q: *What's the difference between "successful" people by society's standards and those seeking transcendence?*

Nobody's opinion matters except your own. What matters is whether or not you're in contact with the core guiding principle of your life. If you don't know what it is, your mission is to find it. When you find it, your mandate is to live by it. If you have betrayed it, then you must go back and reclaim it. And if you are ignoring it, you can only do that for so long before it comes and thumps you on the head. The daemon can be something grand, like serving as the Dalai Lama, or as mundane as being the garbage collector for your city. Only you know how you can best serve.

Q: *Some people may feel that they've found the career that best suits them, so they think they've found their daemon. But for me it's something intangible.*

When you use your career as a means to learn the lessons of life, then it does serve as your daemon. It's the rudder on your boat to help you navigate life's seas, which can be choppy at times. It gives you the disciplined attention you need in order to learn. However, if you're caught up in seeking status or security, your career could merely be busy work to keep *you* in play.

Your daemon may also be the pursuit of truth or wisdom. It could be music or art, or you could be a Renaissance person with a wide variety of interests. If music is your calling, then the study and practice and development of music is the form the daemon would take. You're basically doing the same thing regardless of whether you're a Buddhist monk or a musician—you're learning to transcend your conditioning and realize your oneness with everyone and everything.

The Inner Journey Begins

At what point do you trade in your life vision? When does the sand start to cover the rocks? Your mid-twenties is when you realize that you're not going to get by on youthful charm and wit or good looks; you're paid to do a job. Economic necessity overpowers your dream, and your daemon slowly withers and dies as you busy yourself in your day-to-day life. By the time you're middle-aged, you become bitter, or you bury yourself in the lives of your children or in material things—houses, boats, bank accounts, and concerns about whether you can afford to go to the Caribbean on holiday.

If you are called to the spiritual life, you see the dilemma you're facing, which is—"I have to take care of business, but I have to keep the daemon alive." And you do this by going inward. You shift from outer explorations—traveling the world, having wild sexual encounters, and whatever else you do in your twenties and thirties—to an inner journey. You still work in society and make money to pay the bills, but refuse to sell out your spirit.

This means that you can still be a chartered accountant and follow your daemon. But you must be called to numbers. If you don't really love your job, then you should find a new one because your daemon has to come from what you do in your daily life. Otherwise, you're going to become cynical and disappointed.

Q: *People who are already doing something they're very passionate about, for example, pro tennis players, don't need to find their daemon, do they?*

In terms of their professional identity, they're fine. And if they have no drive to look for something beyond that—something deeper, wider—then I say, "Be happy, enjoy your tennis. Next time I'm in town let's play a game." I don't try to convince them to follow a spiritual path because some are called and others aren't. I talk to those who are called. If you have a calling for something more, then you'll find it because when the student is ready, the teacher appears. I say the "teacher," but I don't necessarily mean a human being. It could be a life situation—maybe a woman, after forty years of a miserable marriage, wakes up one day and says, "It's time for me to move on." That's the calling I'm talking about. If you hear the voice and it applies, go further. If it doesn't, walk on.

Another reason it's so difficult to contact the daemon is because of our education. The body and the emotions, basically two-thirds of who you are, are ignored from grade school right through college. You weren't taught anything about the connection between the two. For example, by changing your breath you can change your feelings. Getting up for a stretch or taking a walk around the block can change your mood.

It's not surprising that as adults you don't have very good interpersonal skills. If you had a fight with your colleague at work, are you going to act as if nothing happened? Emotions affect you, but they have no value in the workplace—it's just, "Get the job done." Of course, you want to be able to do a good job at work, but to do so you must be clear. Getting clear means recognizing what you're feeling in the moment and communicating it to others so you're not carrying it around with you like an old, forgotten tuna fish sandwich.

Several years ago, a famous American university created a "destruction room" on campus. They gathered old furniture and charged students a dollar to go in with a baseball bat and demolish old pianos and chairs. As a result, these students' grade point averages improved. The emotions and the body need space to dialogue. If you want to be authentic, you have to contact the whole gamut of emotions, from apathy and anger to excitement and joy.

The process of finding the daemon is a long journey. Granted, there are exceptions. Carl Sagan, the astronomer, received a very direct message. As a child he loved to look at the stars. Then, when he was twelve, he discovered that he could actually earn a living by studying them; he thought he'd died and gone to heaven. This is unusual, though. So, if you don't know what your daemon is be at peace because the vast majority of other people don't either. One way to get closer to your true purpose is by taking challenges. These new experiences trigger your mind to open doors of new possibilities for you.

Q: *Doesn't positive change often emerge through tragedy?*

Yes, the loss of a job, a bankruptcy, a divorce, the death of a loved one, or a major accident can be an impetus for growth. If you're really out of touch, sometimes the daemon will manifest as a serious disease, to say, "Whoa, you're going the *wrong way!*" Being a high-powered CEO may be good for one woman, but not for another. Chronic fatigue syndrome mostly strikes driven, alpha-type women. The women I know who suffer from this disease say that it made them question their priorities and lifestyle.

Q: *Earlier, you mentioned a woman who woke up after forty years of marriage and realized that she had to leave. Is it possible that forty years earlier she felt she had to marry the guy she did?*

Absolutely. But that's the price of following your daemon. It calls you to constantly change rather than to just snuggle down and get comfortable. However, most people are very attached to results— they feel it doesn't matter how they get there, as long as they get the promotion, or the spouse, or the gold watch at retirement. But following the daemon brings you greater joy, and the difficulties of life don't bother you nearly as much. You don't get caught in the same dumb traps as before because it just says, "It's not your path, sweetheart, get out of here."

Q: *Don't people sometimes wake up temporarily and then go back to sleep?*

Yes, you see this when disaster strikes. People help each other out, whereas a week before, they wouldn't have even talked to each other. In these situations the immediacy of life is brought to bear. It's a fragile thing; you can lose your life at any time.

After 9/11, a massage therapist from New Jersey offered bodywork to the firefighters and the police for a full week. He talked about what an incredible experience it was to give so freely. That's the key—giving freely, without looking to see what you'll get back in return. The disaster takes precedence over the normal discourses of life—"Well, I'm not going to do anything, they didn't do that for me....I'm not going to talk to her because...."

However, the minute things start to move back to normal, what happens? You start to go back to sleep. This is why in monasteries there are no soft chairs or couches. It's not because they are sadists; it's because they understand the nature of the daemon—if you get too comfortable you go to sleep. The danger of modern society is getting too comfortable. It's just too easy to settle down, busy yourself with raising kids, grow old, watch the sunset and die without discovering your purpose for being here.

My teacher was one of the few people I've known who would intentionally put himself in difficult circumstances. He could do this because he had transcended the idea of an ego that is subject to suffering. He used these occasions to demonstrate that it's okay to be inconvenienced and use the struggle to learn something.

Q: *What if that little voice tells you to do something that is in conflict with family and friends or colleagues at work?*

That's a good question. Basically, it's not an easy one. You may have to just go for it—"Goodbye! I'm off. I don't mean to hurt you, but I have no choice. My daemon is calling me." Otherwise, it'll be the death of you. If they truly love you, they'll support you. And if you really love them, you'll leave without resentments.

If your marriage or partnership doesn't end in a spirit of love, life is going to call you back to a similar scenario in the future to do it right the second time. Doing it right means you respond in a friendly and supportive way, no matter what's been done to you. If not, you must come back and meet it again.

This is the reason why the world is a wholesome, positive place; it keeps giving you an opportunity to get it right. If you fail 600 times, it'll still give you another opportunity. So, get it right the first time, which is—love and walk on. If your partner goes with you, it's a bonus. And if you have to leave him or her behind, say, "May you be well and happy, have a good life, hope to see you again."

Now remember, the daemon won't be an "I GOTTA GET OUT OF HERE!" voice. And if it says, "I can't go, I can't go," that's not it, either. The daemon's voice is quiet and resolute—"This is what I must do." Your life was never supposed to stay the same. The daemon says, "This is for now; this works here," which could mean that a relationship lasts sixty or seventy years if it continues to suit both people's daemons and wills.

Q: *There's the screaming "I GOTTA GET OUT OF HERE!" voice and then there's the quieter "Time to go" voice. If you left because of the one that was screaming, how do you get back to your daemon?*

Well, as I said before, you'll end up in a similar situation. But what you're learning is how to recognize the false voice from the true one; this is the main purpose of life anyway. In my case, I worked many summers in the Canadian Arctic so I could travel with my teacher in the winter. Every summer I resented going back up North because it was a surreal world—an Inuit community of a hundred people, no friends, nothing to do, so I spent a lot of time alone. Meanwhile, many of my friends and associates were doing interesting things in other places and I was stuck in the Arctic. I didn't really want to keep working there, but my daemon said, "Make money so you can be with your teacher." So that's what I did.

When I started spending less time with my guru, I continued to work up North out of habit. I got to the point where I *really* didn't want to be there. Then, my last year there my whole view changed; I said, "Yeah, this is fantastic! I could live here forever." I wasn't talking myself into it; I'd made my peace with it. Then my daemon said, "You're finished here."

The daemon doesn't care whether or not you like it. *You* care whether or not you do. Your daemon cares if you've learned something or not. If you run, it will just haul you back until you learn what you're supposed to learn. The good news is that once you begin listening to your daemon you can learn things very quickly. But it doesn't speak categorically. It might say, "Okay, this part of your life is good enough; you can just stay the course there. But for this other area, it's time to try something different." So, in the case of the woman thinking about leaving her marriage, she might stay, but take on the challenge of becoming economically self-sufficient.

Q: *Is listening to the daemon the same as the spiritual path?*

Yes, it's just another word for it. If you don't like "daemon," you can use "Buddha" or "Christ" or whatever you like. The principle is paramount—follow your passion and use your life experiences in conjunction with meditation and guidance from an awakened master to develop a radiant, clear, loving consciousness. Then you won't get buried by the sand—the guilt world or the pressure world or whatever little spook comes to haunt you.

For more resources on the topic of strengthening your personal vision, visit planetdharma.com/dare/resources.

CHAPTER

5

LIVING WELL, LETTING GO:
Four principles of spiritual development

D ISCIPLINE, NON-ATTACHMENT, CHALLENGE, AND COMMUNITY are four principles you need in order to develop spiritually. If you think about discipline in regard to meditation, you might ask yourself a simple question— why don't I practice? Probably it's because it doesn't seem to be effective. If you have a choice between staying home on a Saturday night and meditating or going dancing, what will you most likely do? You're going to choose dancing because you get an immediate endorphin rush—like you do when you eat chocolate or drink beer. Our modern culture reinforces this pleasure-seeking. Everyone we see on TV or in the movies is driving red convertibles along ocean drives or hanging out with friends in bars and cafes. They're not at home struggling with differential calculus or fumbling through the scales on the piano.

What you're being fed by the media is an insidious lie which says that pleasure makes you happy. You may get a quick fix by fulfilling a desire, but the downside is that the satisfaction goes away and you're left with nothing. After the last bite of chocolate cake, your pants don't fit and you get the sugar lows.

Meditation, on the other hand, may seem slow at the beginning, but it's effective. After a session when you go about your business, you feel calmer and clearer. If you go to a retreat and slog away for ten days, it may not seem like you're getting much from it, but you leave feeling recharged. You're more awake, more in tune, and less easily disturbed. Do you feel that way when you leave a dinner party or the movies? Maybe the pleasure lingers for a few minutes but it doesn't last.

Work Is A Capital Good

The happiest people are those who love their work. The Protestant work ethic developed because of a deep-seated understanding that the greatest pleasure in life comes from what you do for a living. While a piece of chocolate cake or a movie is a dead-end consumer product, your work is a capital good—an investment of time and energy which will reward you with calm and joy. Going to the movies or out for a beer is fine, but you should work ninety percent of the time. Pleasure should be a reward to let the muscles you've developed at work take a rest. Similarly, you should only practice meditation six days a week. You need the seventh day to assimilate what you've experienced so that you can approach the practice again in a fresh way.

What you need for spiritual and professional growth—and they are the same in the end—is *samaya*, or "discipline." A disciplined consciousness remains clearly present in all circumstances. This means that when disturbing emotions such as irritation or anxiety surface, you cut them off with mantra, visualization, the breath, or whatever meditative tool you're using. Through this work your concentration gradually gets better and your calm becomes deeper. When you get up from the cushion to cook dinner or go to work, you carry the calm and concentration with you.

This discipline isn't something being forced upon you, but something you choose for yourself. It's different from the idea of discipline you developed in childhood, which was something you were told you should or shouldn't do: "Pee in the toilet. Brush your teeth. Don't throw your food on the floor. Practice the piano." You understandably rebelled against your parents, particularly as a teenager. However, in the process of overthrowing their control, you also tended to deny the merits of discipline.

When you do apply discipline by concentrating on the task at hand, whether it be reciting a mantra and visualizing a deity, balancing the books, or attending a meeting, you won't fall prey to the ego's shenanigans. Nor will you be drawn into the negative states of others. You certainly won't think solely about the paycheck at the end of the month.

Charting Your Course

The return on your investment in meditation is based on your intention. Many people meditate to become calm and peaceful. This is beneficial but it can also be a form of escapism. Others take on the more arduous task of clearing unwholesome karma and discovering their true nature. Rather than solely becoming blissful, the question becomes, "How can I become free from being subject to emotional suffering and break through my biased views based on conditioning?" If this is the kind of freedom you want, then you have to chart your course.

Transcendence isn't possible unless you work at it. Toddlers learn to walk only by picking themselves up off the floor and trying again. No matter how many self-help videos they watch or how many professionals they consult, there's no way they're going to learn to walk unless they keep trying. But you're conditioned to expect almost instantaneous success. If you want growth, you have to put pleasure where it belongs—on the back burner, ten percent of the time, as a medicine, not a lifestyle.

If you do this on a consistent basis, your daemon will come knocking at your door. When you don't know what your calling is, it's because your highest motivation is to get pleasure or avoid struggle. If this is the case, the daemon will remain silent; it only calls when you stop rebelling against discipline.

Embracing Radical Change

The First Noble Truth the Buddha declared was, "Life is struggle." Struggle is not necessarily referring to pain; it's pointing to the fact that everything is constantly changing, which to the ego is absolutely threatening. The ego doesn't want anything to change except what it programs in. But if you're alive to spiritual growth, you must embrace change and accept being threatened at the ego level.

There's no way around it. The ego has its walls in place by the time you're five years old. There's another major upset when you reach puberty; the dramatic physiological changes impact who you think you are. However, this is the last major one in your lifetime. By the time you're in your early to mid-twenties, you have integrated this transformation and have more or less learned to live with your sexuality. From about twenty-five on, you just cement in your identity.

Of course, the ego wants cosmetic changes—you'll change your hair color or get your teeth fixed, maybe give up law and take up medicine.

But these changes don't touch the ego at all. However, the law of spiritual growth demands revolutionary change. If you embrace it, your motivation increases at a time when most people are going to sleep.

What Really Interests Me?

People have difficulty identifying their daemon because they're educated to produce a product. The real purpose of education should be to wake people up to their calling, which then becomes a lifelong pursuit. If you're an artist or a writer, your main purpose is to be fully engaged in the process of painting or writing. Likewise, if you're an architect or an engineer, the end result is secondary. The main point is to be present moment to moment, in the process. A person who learns this lesson becomes a Frank Lloyd Wright or a Jean Sibelius or a Georgia O'Keeffe—people whose work you remember long after they're gone.

The more you let go into the daemon principle, the more rewards *and* struggles it brings you; it's like opening Pandora's Box. If you challenge one aspect of your cultural conditioning, you're likely to challenge more; people will begin to think you're "different." For example, say a young Japanese woman decides to become a doctor. After she graduates, she then decides to move to Calcutta and set up a clinic for underprivileged women, and on and on it goes.

If you listen in quiet times when you're not busy with ego concerns, your daemon will tell you what you should do. But it's not always what you want to hear. It might say, "You've got to get off the couch and get some exercise," or "Okay, you've been drinking too much. It's time to spend less time at the bar." There's no way around it if you're choosing to grow. Of course, you're not growing all the time; most of the time the daemon is pretty quiet, but every few months it beckons. The motivation is always for expansion, which implies a struggle. Without discipline, you might hear the daemon but say, "Oh, I can't, not right now, maybe later." Six months later it will come again and you might tell it to go away. If you continually reject it, it will get quieter and quieter until eventually it will stop talking to you at all in this lifetime.

You need to be honest with yourself—you're not going to sit on the couch, read a novel, watch TV, have three glasses of wine, and then be in contact with the daemon. The only way you'll get a stronger sense of it is through your discipline. You must be quiet and receptive to the clear space your focused mind opens up before you.

An Invitation To Let Go

This brings me to the second principle—letting go. When you choose to let go of something, you almost always get something better instead. It seems like a sacrifice from the ego's point of view, but really it's an invitation for a new and better understanding to emerge. One way or another, life will eventually take away all of your security in the end—your last and most precious thing being your body. However, insofar as you let go of the status quo, the daemon says, "Right, we've got a live one, a human being who wants to be authentic."

This is not just about exuberance. You do have a guiding light and a direction determined by your motivation. Discipline gives you the strength to sacrifice what you have now in order to discover something new. If you don't have the discipline, you won't have the containment field—the scaffolding set up around your building to sustain the walls while it goes through its renovations.

Using Challenges To Grow

The third principle to develop spiritually is accepting challenges. You have to train yourself to respond to the voice of the daemon, and you do so by stepping out on a limb. As I have mentioned before, the formula is: once a week, something easy; once a month, something difficult; and once a year, something seemingly impossible—right over the top for your ego. It needs to be basically wholesome, not cruel or mean, but definitely outside of the realm of your ego's comfort zone. The rest of the time just do business as usual—maintain your practice and keep your attention, but don't think about growing. The stability will allow you to integrate the previous challenge and give you the confidence to step up to the next one.

So, can anybody identify a good weekly challenge? What is something that's easy, but that you wouldn't do unless you set your intention to do it?

Q: How about not drinking coffee?

No coffee for a day. How about next week? Can you use the same challenge twice? No. There are tons of them. Get up an hour earlier! That's a big one. For some of you, that's a yearly challenge. A yearly challenge, by the way, doesn't mean you do it all year; you just do it once. Jump out of an airplane…with a parachute. (You want to be around to do next year's challenge!)

Q: I was thinking more about breaking a pattern, doing something in a new way. So if it's getting up an hour earlier, shouldn't I do it every day for a month?

No, if you do a challenge over and over again it becomes a kind of prison, like being on a diet. What usually happens when you're on a diet is you do it religiously for a week or two and then fall off because you're not really meant to live on a diet; you're supposed to eat what you want.

So you just do it once—one week, no coffee for a day; next week, no cigarettes for a day. You can go the other way too—the following week, three cups of coffee. You want a glass of wine? Drink the whole bottle! "But I don't want to drink the whole bottle." Well, who said it's about what *you* want—it's a challenge! Of course, if you want to drink the whole bottle, then none for you. Other examples?

A: *Doing nothing.*

Can anybody actually do nothing for an hour? That might be a monthly challenge—don't iron, don't rearrange the furniture, don't water the plants, don't think about what you'd like to be doing. I mean literally do nothing! It's very, very hard to do. That's why one famous Rinpoche said, "Life is short. Life is precious. Do nothing." He didn't actually mean to *do nothing*, but to not get caught up in attachment to results.

Your weekly challenge could also be a "to do" list: get to work half an hour early, stay up late—one day just stay up twenty-four hours, do cartwheels in public, give more money than you feel comfortable with. This last one is great because it rouses all sorts of monsters inside about security.

Taking Up Three Seats On The Train

The Japanese are very good at following rules, so I once challenged a Japanese student to take up three seats on the train. It took her a month to get up the nerve to do it. And when she did, she said she felt like evil incarnate. Later, she asked me, "What's the purpose of this exercise if I just feel bad?" I replied, "What's so bad about occupying three seats?"

"Well, nothing really." So I asked, "Why do you think it's bad?" "Well that's the way I've been conditioned."

By taking challenges you're breaking out of the prison of social convention. Of course, you live in society so you should obey its rules most of the time. Still, every once in a while you need to exercise your human spirit by doing something else.

Monthly Challenges

How about once-a-month challenges? Is there something a little bit more difficult than not having coffee one morning or getting up an hour earlier? Does your mind hit a wall? Is it that you can't think of anything, or that you don't want to be seen in your underwear? How about being really nice to someone at work who gets on your nerves? Or being honest and saying what you really think? I'm not trying to create conflict, but rather eliminate the idea that your well-being depends on things being a certain way. Only you know what qualifies as a weekly or monthly challenge—nude modeling for an art class might be a challenge for some of you. So, as you can see, it's very personal.

The point of the challenges is that by meeting them your daemon wakes up. It doesn't matter whether you jump out of an airplane or model for an art class. The key is your willingness to transcend the ego's need for security and comfort. In other words, are you willing to be disturbed? It's not masochism. The purpose is to see outside the parameters of your life. Spending an entire day alone, associating with people you don't normally associate with—these actions send a message to the daemon that you're ready to move on.

Then you'll be faced with the *real* challenge. The ones we've mentioned here are somewhat contrived. The daemon's challenge will be much quieter and gentler; it will make a very subtle impression in your being. It may be something you don't want to do or something that you haven't thought about; it could be something you actually always wanted to do, but could never summon the courage to do.

Embracing Community

The last principle for living well is participating in a community. If you don't belong to a group, you can hide out and pretend to have things integrated that aren't because nobody's there to challenge you. Your peers know when you're pretending and when you're putting on airs. The ego is afraid it's going to be suffocated, drowned, controlled, or otherwise lost in a group. But avoiding community makes you feel isolated. In order to transcend that fear, you need to be part of a group.

You may have left your hometown or your country because of your unconventional views. But why are these views a problem? Because of the pressure to conform. So, what are you avoiding? Pressure! You cannot be a warrior on the spiritual path as long as you avoid it. By avoiding community you can pretend the pressure doesn't exist, but that won't free you. You must join in, be yourself, take the hits, and keep going. If you don't call each other on your blind spots, your spiritual growth will stagnate, no matter how much meditation you do.

Q: *Do you have any suggestions on how to deal with the pressures of community?*

Nobody has the power to upset your state of mind. You put the most pressure on yourself by needing others' approval. You have to discover what monster is enslaving you. For some, it's the fear of being seen as a fool or a loser. For others, it's the fear of being fired, ostracized, or winding up homeless. Your peers just intensify the speed with which you see your own patterns. So use each other.

This is why people join monasteries—there's no home to run to where you can close the door and say, "Thank God! I have until tomorrow morning to put my ego back together." In a spiritual community you don't get that privilege...or escape. You are present all day, every day.

That's why your discipline is so important. It gives you the breathing room to deal with the intensity of the community, meet challenges, and stay cool. If you don't have control over your mind, you can't do it. This is why every spiritual teaching since the dawn of humankind has had practices to steady the mind—mantras or prayers or making bread or sweeping the walks. That discipline isn't supposed to be a prison; it's supposed to be a room you can learn to let go in.

You must show up for each other honestly and with real heart. There was a point in your life when you needed to run. But you've done that already. You can't keep running. It's time to stop, turn around, and meet whatever you're afraid of. You can do it gently most of the time. But you have to meet it. The reason you don't go to the mat with anybody else is so that you don't have to face your shadow reflected in them—"I'll leave you alone if you leave me alone," and thus, you feel… alone.

Q: *How do you know when to confront someone and when to just leave them alone?*

You check in with your heart. When you see someone struggling, ask yourself what is the more loving thing to do? Point something out? Not necessarily. It might be to leave her alone. The daemon will tell you if you ask, but if your ego position is to point things out, then you're going to, whether it's skillful or not. If you ask the daemon, you'll act from the heart. One day it will tell you to point something out, and the next day it will say, "Leave it alone." And that won't necessarily have anything to do with the message you're getting from the other person, which might be, "Leave me alone."

If you're in touch with the daemon, you'll know how to respond. Rather than two egos squaring off, your open interaction will become the mandala of self and other—the totality of both of you.

For more resources on the topic of living well and establishing supportive structures, visit planetdharma.com/dare/resources.

CHAPTER

6

THE HUNGRY EGO:
Creating space between yourself and your objects

Whenever we were boys in the Canadian Prairies, we used to play a game where we would grab each others' nipples, squeeze, twist, and say "Whistle!" The only way we could manage to do it was to breathe into the pain and find our calm first. As soon as we whistled, the other kid would let go. The truth of the matter is that life is a squeezed nipple. There's no way around it. Some of you are feeling the effects of getting older—your vision isn't what it used to be, or your bones are aching. This is not going to get any better in the long run. You can't avoid the decay of the body or the struggles of life, but you can always have access to luminosity and bliss. First, however, you have to get past the negative or conflicting emotions that are your response to the nipple squeeze and find your whistle. Your choice is to either struggle and be in pain or accept and let go. If you can choose the latter, then consciousness is no longer tied to the pain; it naturally returns to the clear mind.

According to Eric Berne, author of *Games People Play*, there are three hungers that drive the human ego: the needs for stimulation, structure, and recognition. These three interdependent hungers motivate our social interactions and keep the ego feeling in charge. However, feeding them keeps us away from luminosity and bliss.

Stimulation

The hunger for stimulation relates to our basic survival; it's our need for contact. If you don't have stimulation, you'll seek it out, and if you can't find it, you'll create your own. The classic example is to put a yogi in a cave and seal it up with concrete blocks, leaving only a little opening at the bottom to put in a bowl of rice and take out the chamber pot. What's going to happen to the mind in this situation? It will start to hallucinate—seeing monsters, devils, and angels. It's like looking through old photo albums—the memories start flooding in.

Leonard Cohen wrote a song with the line, "There is a crack in everything; that's how the light gets in." The crack in your mind is to let bliss in. But we are conditioned to seek it in objects rather than in the spaces between them. For instance, what do you see when you look at me?

A: *A guy with a blanket around him, holding a necklace.*
[He is wearing a traditional Buddhist robe and holding a Buddhist rosary.]

Exactly, but what do you see in the space between your eyes and mine? If, rather than being the "observer" that sees the "object," you see the space between you and me, then you are very close to bliss. It's like that Psychology 101 drawing of two faces and a vase. You'll notice either the faces or the vase, though both are clearly present. If you look at the image long enough, or someone points it out to you, you will see both.

Likewise, in any observation it's important to keep an eye on the space, or emptiness, inherent to it. Bliss lies in the space, but the nature of the ego consciousness is to go straight to the object.

At deeper levels of meditative concentration the object drops out entirely. These states are referred to in Buddhist terminology as the *arupa jhanas*, or "formless realms of absorption." This is where bliss moves into luminosity. Using a metaphor, bliss is admiring a lily, while luminosity is looking at an x-ray of the flower. At this higher vibration all that is present is pure perception; you transcend the object and the observer gradually disappears.

Structure

The second hunger is for structure, the drive to organize experience. This includes personal and communal rituals, work, pastimes, and relationships. Personal rituals are usually calming and peaceful. For example, most of us have a morning ritual. My thing is to get up, go to the bathroom, put my clothes on, and then lurk over the coffee machine in the kitchen. Finally, I grab my coffee and I'm ready to be a Dharma teacher. We do our thing repetitively because it's comfortable; it gives us a sense that our day is humming along nicely.

It's very interesting to observe what happens to consciousness when you disrupt your rituals because you're stepping outside of your comfort zone. If you can still maintain your refuge in bliss and clarity, then any interference with your habits won't faze you. You don't have to eliminate your rituals, but every once in a while—on a good day when you don't have any big meetings or millions of dollars on the line—change your pattern and watch what happens.

While personal hot drink rituals are comforting to the individual, they're also extremely important for a community. Communal rituals are the social structure we impose on our lives to try to understand them. Some people go to church, temple, or AA meetings because these rituals give them a feeling of community.

Generally speaking, however, today's multicultural societies lack group rituals. Team sports, like baseball or soccer, connect the community in a way, but they're mere pastimes—our team versus their team. When the Toronto Blue Jays won the World Series, the Americans were upset because a non-American team won. The general manager of the Blue Jays responded by saying, "Our Dominicans beat their Dominicans."

Church or temple rituals, on the other hand, call one to the higher motivation of love, truth, and wisdom. However, people who don't go to church regularly or engage much in the ceremony could be using it as a pastime. What elevates an activity to the level of ritual is the participants' commitment and focused attention.

A darker aspect of community rituals is to create a scapegoat. This happens especially among native peoples. In some small towns in the Himalayas, for example, if things don't go well for extended periods of time, the whole town agrees that the problems are somebody's fault and that person is banned from the village. After some months, when things improve, the scapegoat returns and is welcomed back with open arms. If things begin to go badly again, a new scapegoat is nominated, and on it goes. This is a very sane approach, relatively speaking, to relieving tension in a group and maintaining cohesion.

It works the same way for the ego. The scapegoat for all of a person's problems will most likely be a parent—"I didn't get enough love and attention; she didn't do this, he didn't do that." If they don't choose a parent, they'll pick somebody else. The last scapegoat is oneself; very few people think, "It's my fault, I'm no good, I can't do anything." Even someone in the throes of self-hate will usually blame their mom for it. Self-hate is totally narcissistic—you hate yourself and you're unhappy about it. It's a stubborn refusal to engage in anything that would improve your self-esteem.

Q: *What's the difference between having a healthy ego and being self-centered?*

All egos are self-centered; ego, by definition, means separation and isolation. But it doesn't make sense to talk about not having an ego because you wouldn't be human without one; human consciousness is the great separator. You need an ego to function in the world—to explore, to make decisions. The question is whether the ego is your servant or your master. As a servant, it can exercise its discriminating function. However, if discrimination degenerates into judgment, then the ego has become the master; it forgets that it's part of a community where each ego is okay just as it is. But it's a mixed bag. At times the ego exercises a wholesome discriminating function, and at other times it acts judgmentally and isolates itself. This is why awakening takes so long. When egos are engaged in positive exploration rather than aching to be acknowledged, they can get along with other egos much more easily.

The next question becomes, "What am I going to do with my time?" For most people work provides the greatest structure to their lives and gives them their strongest sense of identity. Still, luminosity and bliss are not *inherent* in a particular line of work. No matter whether one is a doctor or a ditch-digger, these radiant states will be present if you discipline yourself moment to moment while on the job.

Take the example of a composer. Bliss and clarity are not the result of composing; instead, you are channeling bliss into music and then out into the world. However, you may be missing the clarity in order to be successful. If you get caught up in evaluating your performance or cherishing your status, you lose luminosity. Then the ego moves to pride because now it has to either defend or promote itself. This indicates where you are taking refuge. Beware, because this false refuge is a dangerous one—if you lose your ability to write music, your self-esteem will collapse. But if the ego isn't taking its refuge in work or anything else, luminosity can never be lost.

The deepest level of structure in which the ego seeks fulfillment is to be involved in an intimate relationship. Most people feel that intimacy is the highest form of bliss they can experience. However, they don't really want it for more than a short time. Why? Because it's full on! It requires you to be absolutely present, absolutely there. The ego always backs away from it. After a moment of intimacy, you say, "Let's go for a walk." I don't just mean sexual intimacy, but any kind of heart-to-heart meeting, sexual or not.

Recognition

The third hunger, the hunger for recognition, is the need to have your existence acknowledged by others. We seek to fulfill this hunger by being handsome and charming, powerful and intelligent, athletic—any label we put on ourselves to get emotional feedback from others. We fool ourselves with these labels instead of recognizing that bliss and luminosity, which are independent of ego, are what really give life meaning. You can see this with athletes, politicians, and business executives—when their world collapses or changes, they crumble.

An ego's need to be recognized can be compared to a baby bird that falls from the nest. Its first response is to squawk, "Mommy, mommy, I'm here! Come get me!" But if the mother bird doesn't respond quickly enough, the chick knows instinctively that if it's too noisy, predators will find it, so then it becomes very quiet. If it waits too long, however, it's going to die. Now it must risk attracting the predator in order to get its mother's attention because it won't survive without her.

Like the baby bird, your ego has also been designed to make noise. The easiest way for most children to be recognized is by being good. However, if that doesn't work, they'll misbehave to get some sort of attention. Eventually, the persistent lack of recognition could cause them to go insane because this need is so basic.

Happiness Is Your Intrinsic State Of Being

Generally, this is how you live your life—looking for fulfillment in objects. In order to find refuge in bliss and clarity, you have to let go of the idea that a career, a relationship, or anything else will satisfy or save you. There is no refuge to be found in *any* object anywhere. Of course, luminosity and bliss are not objects either. Words define them, but in directly experiencing them there are neither words nor objects.

You might argue that your highest motivation is for happiness. Well, I would argue that happiness is your intrinsic state of being if you're dwelling in luminosity. But, alas! You let the hunger for stimulation, structure, and recognition blind you—pulling your attention toward *your* way of seeing things. You then lose bliss by arguing relentlessly for your point of view. However, if you catch on to how this happens, you are forewarned in how not to be fooled. So, forget happiness. Happiness is none of your business! Your business is to remain in a state of clarity no matter what's going on.

Q: *Is it possible to have both bliss and the object?*

Absolutely, but you need to choose bliss first. Through the process of meditation you establish a "witness" to the experience; it's this witness or observer who chooses the bliss. But the observer is still attached to an object by putting limits and edges on it. Observation, in effect, inhibits a sense of spaciousness. The stickiest part, in terms of gaining freedom from ego-clinging, is that this witness claims that the observations are its *own*. From this sense of ownership, likes and dislikes are quickly formed and *sunyata*, "emptiness" or "spaciousness," is lost. So, having seen the inherent emptiness of the observation, you have to also see the inherent emptiness of the observer. Then you've completed the loop.

It's not the case that anything has to be given up. You don't have to stop having dialogues with other people or participating in society. Your life continues much as it did before. The only difference is that you're not fooled into thinking that any activities can, in and of themselves, produce luminosity. Instead, you know that luminosity lies in the gap between things.

Q: *Do you have to recognize that none of it matters?*

Everything matters completely and totally. In order to manifest loving-kindness, you have to be 100% engaged. Life is a play, and the ego's function is to explore, discover, and make choices on its stage. At the same time you must not be attached to the results. Be careful, though, because too much equanimity could be masking indifference.

Following A Spiritual Map

People on a spiritual path need to realize that there's a big difference between having a very good map to Toronto and actually getting in the car and going there. Many people understand the map, but whether they actually get in the car and head down the road is another thing.

This teaching becomes more visceral when you throw yourself in the ocean and go scuba diving or go up in a plane and skydive. It's all well and good to say luminosity and bliss are present, but can you strap the parachute on your back and leap? The actual spiritual life is leaping—putting yourself in a situation where you're experiencing it totally—staying alone in a cabin for ten days to see whether the bliss remains. The challenges are crucial.

As soon as you let objects fool you, bliss is gone. Arguments over differing views show how stubborn we are—"This is the way it is," or "My way or the highway." Most conflicts, however, stem from the need to be recognized—"Do you see me? Am I being acknowledged?" To entertain clarity and bliss, you must be willing to drop all views and emotions.

It's a sure sign that the ego is speaking when you lose the luminous state of mind during conflicts. Luminosity cannot be interfered with by arguments, war, hatred, murder, or death. The practice is to maintain bliss no matter what challenge is presented to you. You don't have to feel bad when you've lost it—you just have to acknowledge it. Admit that you're not in a state of luminosity, and, therefore, the ego is dominating. If you're honest about it, then you have a choice. You can either get caught up in frustration and argument or you can return to luminosity and bliss. Which will you choose?

For more resources on the topic of creating more wholesomeness in your life, visit planetdharma.com/dare/resources.

CHAPTER 7

THE KEYS TO THE PALACE:
The five faculties and five hindrances

That you are conscious is the most salient fact of your existence. This is what makes you human. You have a consciousness that is vast—much, much bigger than you give it credit for. It's like a huge generating plant, and you're only taking advantage of a tiny fraction of the energy available.

It reminds me of a famous Sufi story about a king who lives in squalor in the dungeon of his palace. Imagine a king choosing to stay in the dungeon surrounded by rats and dirt when he's been given the keys to the palace. You are just like the king. Above you are immense, gorgeous rooms called "Exploration of the Universe," and yet you choose to ignore them.

The reason for this passivity is you've been conditioned not to leave the dungeon. It's as simple as that. You've been told, "Don't leave the basement. If you do, you're going to go crazy. It's dangerous and you're going to die." But the bigger fear is that nobody will love you. This last point clinches it: you do not want to be alone.

Meanwhile, down in the dungeon, you're busy entertaining yourself.

You are an addict. Again and again you get diverted from your higher purpose and go back to sleep. Occasionally, little messages float down from upstairs—"There's something more." Your response is, "Yeah, yeah, I'm busy right now. I'm cooking." Again you hear, "There's something more!" "I know but I have to pay the bills." Or, "The pipes are leaking and I have to fix them before I can go upstairs and look around." Before you know it, you're sixty, seventy, eighty, and then somebody asks you, "Hey, did you ever actually go upstairs and look around the palace?" "Well, I intended to, but no… I never quite got around to it."

The Key To Freedom

The key to freedom from life in the palace basement is a thorough understanding of our shared conditioning. If you're Canadian, you share Canadian conditioning. If you're female, you share female conditioning, and so on. While individuals in your group aren't identical, there's still a lot of similarity. If you're in your thirties, that puts you in the 1970s room of the palace dungeon. If you're in your fifties, you belong to the 1950s room. Everyone looks around their conditioned rooms and thinks, "This is all there is—what you see is what you get."

The purpose of meditation is to get a little key into a little lock to open the door to freedom. It brings your attention out of the basement and starts to focus the mind on other things: peace, clarity, compassion, and wisdom. Transcendence doesn't mean you stop living in the world. You can still have your bed in the basement, but over time you will move upstairs. Jesus said, "My father's mansion has many rooms." He offered humanity the entire palace. This doesn't mean the basement is bad, but that there's more air and light above. If you had the choice between a basement apartment and a penthouse, which would you choose? You'd take the penthouse, of course!

There is no end to the suffering and struggles of life. You need to stop looking for things outside yourself to bring you happiness. Give up hoping again and again that more money or sex, a better job or a better relationship is going to make it all okay. This strategy may work for a while, but eventually it won't because the very mind that seeks happiness in an object is the mind that destroys it.

Have you gone out to buy something new recently? A new shirt? How long does the pleasure last? Until you wash it and it needs ironing. Then you need another hit—that is the struggle of life. But in the palace, you no longer get your happiness from objects. Your happiness comes from the experience of the moment itself, without an object—just the joy of being alive, even as your body begins to rot from underneath you. Lovers come and lovers go, money comes and money goes, life comes and life goes. There is no lasting happiness to be found in the objects of life, important and precious as these things may be.

The trick is not to learn how to avoid struggle—that's impossible. The point is to learn how to be free from being subject to suffering. That's a perfect description of upstairs in the palace. At the top of the stairs the banner reads: *"Here You Are No Longer Subject To Suffering!"*

Now, to be clear, suffering still exists. You're going to get sick and die; people are going to dislike you. But you'll never again take it personally. It's not about you; it's just the process of life.

The awakened consciousness is peaceful because it doesn't take loss or death personally. It doesn't believe in an inherent identity that's subject to suffering. In fact, there is no "you" to be found. There are sensations; there are some thoughts, some feelings, and a few memories kicking around about people you've known. There are some concepts (which you will alter according to the day of the week). As for your body, every seven years every molecule in the body is replaced. At the moment there may be 10,000 Hitler molecules in you, 10,000 Buddha molecules, 10,000 Mars molecules, and 10,000 molecules from the people who died on September 11th. The firefighters, the police officers, and the paramedics were all breathing in vaporized molecules of the dead as they fought the fire. You are cosmic dust! And when you dissolve, everybody will breathe you in.

We hold onto an illusion of a separate, lasting, independent ego that we created as children to protect ourselves from our parents. But it's a mirage. In fact, your cruel slave master does not exist. The slave master is the idea that you are alone, unworthy, unloved, abandoned, and need to fight for something you already have. You've been given the key to the kingdom of heaven. It's yours; it is right here. All you have to do is put the key in the lock and turn it.

The Five Faculties

To get out of the basement you need to summon five faculties, or *indriya*, which in Sanskrit literally means "belonging to Indra." Indra is a chief deity in Hinduism, embodying power and strength. The Five Faculties are faith (*saddha*), energy (*viriya*), concentration (*samadhi*), wisdom (*pañña*), and mindfulness (*sati*).

Faith

The first faculty is faith. You need to believe that there is indeed a palace above your head, that human consciousness does in fact have vast potential. You don't have to believe in Jesus or Buddha. All you need is to believe that there is an experience called liberation and that it's available to you.

It doesn't matter how much money you have or how smart you are; you can't charm your way into the palace. Maybe you think that if you wait long enough, God is going to open the door for you. That's not going to happen. You have to do it yourself. There is no method to achieve transcendence except a leap of faith. You need the faith that it exists, that it is possible to get there, and that you can reside there. You must decide for yourself, "I am going to change my residence. I'm moving out of the basement to live upstairs."

Energy

You need energy to bring your consciousness to bear on the fact that you're locked in the basement. While faith overcomes doubt, energy overcomes inertia, which says, "Well, I don't know. I can't be bothered today. I'm tired. I have a date with my boyfriend. I'll do it later." Precious energy is also wasted on dead-end emotions such as disappointment or resentment. Surrender your disappointment when things don't work out. Surrender your resentment that you've been burned. Then you'll have the energy available for the task at hand—freedom!

Concentration

You've had decades and decades of non-stop action, and when you sit down to meditate you're trying to bring your mind to a sudden stop. Have you ever noticed how long it takes to halt a jumbo jet? It takes a long, long time. Do you really think your mind will go into a state of rest in a few days or weeks? It takes time and patience. And once you understand that the willingness to quiet your mind is in fact the formula for opening the door, then you will be more motivated to persist.

To become peaceful you need to concentrate. You can't allow your mind to wander off. It will, but you've got to bring it back home. Now, you will fail again and again, and many of you might quit. But have you ever met kids who refused to learn to talk because their parents didn't understand their gibberish? So why quit meditating? You've forgotten your childhood perseverance to learn how to talk. And that's exactly what you need.

Jesus said, "Unless you change and become like little children, you will never enter the kingdom of heaven." This doesn't mean you should become childish. It means you should recover the child's innocence, enthusiasm, energy, determination and focus—in this case, for the purpose of learning to sit still with a flower in meditation. You need to sit still in the beginning for only twenty minutes. Just twenty minutes! You easily waste twenty minutes a day. Why not "waste" it meditating and see what happens?

Wisdom

Energy and concentration need to be kept in balance. If you have too much energy, you can't focus. And if the concentration is too strong, it's easy to slip into dullness. Similarly, faith gets balanced with wisdom. You must examine your experience directly, not take someone else's word for it.

You gain wisdom by being concentrated, energetic, having faith and applying your mind to the nature of reality. This is where it gets very difficult because in order to have the faith to meditate, you need the wisdom to see the end result of all your actions. And you also must have enough life experience to recognize that you're not going to find happiness in objects.

This is not a denial of the material world, as it is often misinterpreted, but just a statement about where your well-being lies. The things in the basement are impermanent. They are subject to change. They are subject to loss and in a constant state of struggle. There is no peace to be found there.

This is a hard lesson. You keep trying again and again to find satisfaction in objects. But it has never worked and it never will. Happiness lies within your *state*, and your state depends upon your ability to let go of the idea that all those objects are going to make you happy.

Mindfulness

As the first four faculties develop, offering greater states of calm and clarity, they become powers. Your awareness becomes more lucid and you're no longer fooled by the advertising. You come to the stark realization that you are alone. No matter how close you bring another person to you, you're still alone. When you embrace this reality, you understand that the person sitting next to you is also totally alone. Now, if you can both drop your ego positioning, your minds can open up into spaciousness. All of us share the seed of transcendence because we're human. Awakened beings experience every worry, every hope, every struggle and fear, but they don't take these things personally. There's no room in transcendence for "you" or "me."

But first you need faith to get you to the meditation cushion and energy to keep you there. Mindfulness is the umbrella over them all. It protects the mind against agitation and idleness. Even if you get cancer, it won't have the power to disturb your state of mind, as long as you don't get caught by thinking things should be different.

The Five Hindrances

The obstacles to your practice are called The Five Hindrances. What you need to get out of the basement is to just ride them out.

Sense Desire

The first obstacle you meet when you start meditating is *kama-chanda*, usually translated as "sense desire." *Kama* means "desire" and *chanda* means "moon," so *kama-chanda* literally means "wishing for the moon." In other words, you want something that isn't present—such as a feeling of harmony—to be present; or you want something that *is* present not to be—such as the person smoking a cigarette beside you. Perhaps you want peace and quiet but work in a noisy office. Wanting things to be different from what they are is the essence of the first hindrance. There is no other basis for suffering.

Anger And Aversion

The second obstacle is anger. Anger comes up a lot on the cushion. You're quietly meditating in a room and suddenly you get the urge to put your fist through the wall or punch the meditator beside you. Where is this aversion coming from? The feeling is unfocused initially, but eventually you find a target for it—your teacher, your mother, or anybody at all. In any case, just let it pass through.

Sleepiness

If you're persistent, you'll sit through to the next hindrance, sleepiness, which is also called "sloth and torpor." Sleepiness is actually an escape. You might say to yourself, "I can't justify actually quitting because mom said good people don't quit. I mean, how can I fail at doing nothing? On the other hand, the angels aren't singing. I'm just sitting here feeling livid! I won't quit; but I sure am feeling sleepy." And then, after about twenty minutes, you wake up and say, "Oh, what a waste of time!"

Restlessness

Next is when the agitation starts. Many people quit at this point. You wish you could get back to your life. You want to paint the garage or talk to your friends or see what's happening on Facebook. You're addicted to the entertainments of life. You figure that if you don't have them, you're going to miss something—"Oh, I'm just sitting here on the cushion doing nothing and everybody else is out having a good time. They're at the party, they're at the concert. This Buddhism is ridiculous!" You go through all of your fantasies and then the hour is up and you say, "Well, that meditation didn't do anything for me."

In the beginning, meditation is mostly finding out what it's not. It isn't your internal dialogues; it isn't the feelings that arise. Meditation is the process of watching those things become apparent until eventually your whole makeup is revealed—your temper, your jealousy and resentment, as well as your kindness, humor, and honesty. Eventually, you get so tired of the mind bugging you that you start to get upset—"I was expecting Buddha to come down and land on my head and all I'm getting is CNN." Fortunately, the more you practice sitting, the longer you're able to sustain the meditation. Then one day you realize that you haven't thought about yourself in a long time and you say, "Thank God!"

Skeptical Doubt

The last of the hindrances is skeptical doubt—"This isn't getting me anywhere; it's a dead end. I might as well be surfing the Net." You say this because you're used to instant gratification. If you click a link and the page doesn't load immediately, you wonder if it will ever load. When you start doubting, you stop meditating because you think it's not working. But IT IS WORKING! You just need to be patient. If it were easy, everyone would be happy. If meditation doesn't seem easy, it's because, fundamentally, you don't believe in it. You have to be convinced of the possibilities available to you above your head in the palace and then practice.

Life Conspires In Your Favor

If you pay attention, you'll see that you meet the hindrances not only in meditation but also in life. They follow the same pattern. For example, say you're excited about going out on a date. Then, when you finally get there the conversation seems a bit superficial. You're not getting what you want, so you get upset. Then you start feeling tired. You glance at your watch, but you can't leave because it would be rude. Finally, you wonder why you bother dating at all.

There are many obstacles to integrating meditation into your daily life, but once you start, things get easier. As it says in the Bible, "Seek ye first the kingdom of heaven, and all else shall be added unto you." If you actually do this, you will find that life conspires to improve the conditions around you. It is truly magical. I don't know how it works or why it works, but I know it works. Somehow, life manages to support your aspiration to awaken.

For more resources on the topic of understanding how the mind works, visit planetdharma.com/dare/resources.

CHAPTER 8

FISHING IN DEEP WATERS:
Acknowledging the shadows

Having met the teaching, don't start. This ancient warning is your last chance to jump ship while you still can. But having started, don't stop, because the middle ground is unbearable. You won't belong in the world in terms of its conventional values, and you won't really have gotten out of it either. So, if you've started, put your practice in place and forge ahead until the day when you realize that the person you always thought of as "you" doesn't even exist.

In the collection of experiences called "you," there's actually no "you" to be found. In the smell, there's smell. In the sound, there's sound. In the taste, there's taste. In the thought, there's just thought. This realization is a huge tidal wave—from the persona's point of view the biggest that will hit you in your lifetime.

Now, in case you're ready to run for the lifeboats, remember that beyond the tidal wave lies clarity and peace. Every spiritual crisis, every moment of mental anguish, is only one breath away from peace— one breath! Well, okay, masters take three breaths, so you can take a few dozen. However, to experience this peace you have to let go of the belligerent or whiney voices that come up when you start to feel threatened, confused, or needy. You must shift your attention away from trying to manage your world to examining the nature of your reactive patterns. Awareness of your breath helps create the space needed to do so. Then the tidal wave will pass.

If you become aware of what's present in the moment and analyze its structure and fabric, a door of insight opens. For example, suppose you've had an argument with someone, and every time you see him or her, you get irritated. Rather than thinking how you'll tell that person off, move from your thoughts to your body. Notice that your stomach feels tight, your teeth are clenched, and your heart is racing. Bringing your attention to what is present isn't the same as repression or avoidance. The key to letting go is to fully acknowledge how the story is running through your system.

Missing The Mark

The original meaning of the word sin is "to miss the mark." So it isn't necessary to think of sin as bad. Your religion may tell you that if you have sexual thoughts you're a sinner. The important consideration is whether or not those sexual thoughts are taking the place of a wholesome state of mind. When you can recognize what the mind is doing and remain in a harmonious state, then whatever arises, even sexual thoughts, is fine. Jesus said, "I have come that they may have life, and that they may have it more abundantly." He didn't come to bring you celibacy, porridge, cold water, and a toothpick.

With letting go comes a sense of vastness. But it doesn't happen immediately. Even after you've recognized how and where you cling, the release may not occur until you fish a little deeper. Perhaps you've seen the attachment in broad strokes but not in the fine detail, so it's not quite as simple as I've stated.

Let me give you an example of how this plays out in intimate relationships. Say Nicola is mad at Ian because he said her new haircut looked weird. Even though she recognizes that she's reacting to his comment, she still can't drop her anger. If she looked closer she would remember that her mother always told her she had unruly hair. But she's unable to see this because she's so mad at Ian. She can't drop her anger because, in fact, the real issue is her mother's criticism.

If you can't let go of a negative emotion, you don't need to see this as failure. See it as an opportunity to go fishing in deeper water. The mother's rejection of the young girl's appearance was much more powerful than Ian's comment, but rather than face what's buried in her subconscious, it's much easier for Nicola to be upset with her boyfriend. Her persona was built to avoid the fact that she felt her mother didn't love her enough. From a child's point of view, no mother ever does. A mother's job is to teach and correct because she wants her child to be successful in society. The repetition of such experiences creates fear in the child of losing her mother's love.

Liberation is possible when Nicola uncovers what's buried at the bottom of her psyche. The key is to recognize that even if she can't drop it, at least she knows there's gold in them there hills and that she's being presented with an opportunity to go looking for it. Your practice keeps you honest; it's to admit, "I'm not dropping this. I've got to look—maybe not right now—but at the next retreat or the next time I have a few free days. I'm going to put a little flag on this one." Nicola's practice isn't to pretend it never happened and go watch a movie or to break up with Ian.

The reason you tend not to make this effort is because of all the stuff that pours into your life—jobs, relationships, money, politics… You might say emphatically, "I don't have time to look at this!" My argument is that you don't have time not to. If Nicola doesn't reach inside and let go of the pain she's carrying, it will come up again and again. If she gets rid of Ian, she'll get Richard, and if she gets rid of him, she'll get Rosalie and the cycle will continue.

The Sand In The Oyster

Spiritual teachers exist for a reason: you need someone to point out these patterns. Actually, we just drag you into retreat, close the door, and when you say, "Let me out!" we say, "No." But we only do that if you're serious. We don't do that against your will; we do that because you want us to. One of our jobs is to be an irritant, like sand in an oyster. The sand is necessary to produce a pearl, just as pointing out unhealthy patterns is crucial to the awakening process—"Look at this one! You can spend twenty years avoiding it, but here it is, right in front of you. Do you want to wait twenty years or do you want to do it now?" The teacher's life is supposed to be inspirational—to show what's possible, what the fruit of the journey is.

If you say, "I don't want to do it," then I say, "May you have a happy life, good luck, I hope your dreams come true." If you say, "I want to do it but I want to do it slowly," then you see me rarely—maybe give me a telephone call now and again—"Hi, Qapel, how's everything? Goodbye." You don't *have* to go to retreat to acknowledge what's lurking in the shadows of your being. However, the purpose of retreats is to give you a solid block of time in a quiet environment where you can get a bigger push on what's holding you back.

You can do it within the context of a busy family life if you choose to turn your attention to it, but it's difficult. Even if you want to reach deeper levels of your mind, you get distracted. To be mindful in your day-to-day life requires a very strong will. You have to remember that your job is not only to put spaghetti on the table, but also to be aware of the state you're in as you put the spaghetti on the table. Whether you are in retreat or negotiating a multi-million dollar deal, you can train your mind to be in the very same state of calm, active inquiry.

Reclaiming Your Buddha Nature

If you have the aspiration, there is only one outcome to life—transcendence. How can I state that with such assurance? Because that's where you started from! You started as an awakened being but fell asleep. Your parents trained you to function in the world and live with other people; they've completed their duties. Your job is to take that gift—life and the ability to get along in the world—and go back to reclaim your Buddha nature.

The spiritual life begins for people after they have established their autonomy. Once you see yourself as a separate, independent person responsible for your own growth and development, then the aspirant inside you says, "Okay, I've done that but there's still something missing."

In the East, society tries to subsume the person within the group before they've developed a strong personal identity. In Burma and Thailand, for instance, when you are called to join the order, your hair is shaved and you're dressed in a white robe or plain clothes. You sit among a sea of people who are going through the same process, and when it's your turn they say *"nagosa, nagosa,"* which basically means "hey you" or "nobody in particular." It has the same leveling effect as school uniforms. The purpose is to eliminate the personality's positioning. This attempt fails, however, unless one *chooses* to surrender.

My teacher asked me very early on, "Are you willing to be a slave?" I responded, "Absolutely!" And for the next twenty years I basically was. You're not a slave to a person. In fact, there is no cruel slave master in your life—not your boss, your teacher, or your parents. Actually, the only real slave master is your ego, and the guru's job is to point that out to you.

Searching For Keys In The Light

A classic Sufi story about the absurdity of ignoring our blind spots involves the mystic Nasrudin. He'd been out drinking with his friends one night and had returned home. There was just one street light, and Nasrudin's house was over in the dark. His friend came along and saw him crouched on the ground under the street light and asked, "Nasrudin, what are you doing?" The sage replied, "I'm looking for the key to my house." His friend got down on his hands and knees to help. Not finding it, he asked, "Nasrudin, whereabouts do you think you dropped it?" "Over by my house" was his answer. "Then why are we looking here?!" asked his friend. Nasrudin replied, "Well, there's more light here."

The moral of this story is that if you're looking for world peace, environmental healing, or the perpetrator of your abuse, you're looking in the wrong place. You need to look within. The key is found in the awareness of your attachment to transient physical, emotional, and mental states. And if you don't know where to begin, it's okay to ask for help. Ask your friends or your teacher, or lock yourself in a room and don't come out until revelation dawns.

The Door Will Find You

The fundamental issue we face in life is not lack of love or fear of being rejected but *lack of trust*. What takes you to awakening is the belief that the universe is love. Everything that's wrong in the world is because of frightened egos that are out of control. If you trust that we are part and parcel of this loving universe and that awakening is inherent in the human condition, then you don't even have to look for the door. The door will find you. This is a big jump, I'll admit, from the persona's point of view. But saying you can't find the door is like saying, "I don't want to find clear, radiant awareness," or "I looked for fifteen minutes in meditation last week and it didn't show up, so it's probably not there." The persona is very clever at hiding its mistrust. But if you truly trust that the universe is awake, you just dive into that ocean. And it *will* rise to meet you—if not sooner, then later.

Granted there are a lot of used car salesmen out in the world and you might think I'm one of them. Don't trust Doug Duncan. Trust what I represent. You have to decide for yourself whether the universe is a place of love and truth or not. You can't get someone else to do it for you. Get very quiet and listen. If what I'm saying is right, you'll know it. Don't listen to the loud, yappy voices of conditioning that spring up in moments of struggle. Just acknowledge them—"Yes, hi Mum, yes Mother. Uh huh, hi Dad, how are you?" Then wait them out.

Practice awareness. If you can't do it on the meditation cushion, then use your day-to-day experiences as a channel for awakening. You can turn your present situation into your path of practice, and little by little your daemon will tell you what to do next. But you must truly listen. As you trust your daemon more, your commitment will give you the strength for a deeper, wider practice, which will lead you beyond the rough days to bliss and glory.

For more resources on the topic of preparing for and participating in retreats, visit planetdharma.com/dare/resources.

CHAPTER

9

DOCKING THE QE II:
Instructions for meditation retreat

Most of us come into retreat from a busy, active life, which is a bit like trying to dock an ocean liner cruising at top speed. Your Queen Elizabeth II is forging through the ocean and all of a sudden you find yourself in a silent retreat trying desperately to come to a dead stop. Meanwhile, your mind is still processing 10,000 things.

I'd like to give you some instructions on how to enter a state of calm and concentration slowly and easily. Start by using the senses as the basis for your meditation. This practice will ground you in the present moment. For instance, if you start with sight, spend twenty minutes simply observing things. You can switch from object to object during that time—say, from a flower to a tree to the roof, but remember to keep your meditation limited to seeing. After you have worked with the visual sense, go to the next one—for example, smell. Go around sniffing things for half an hour—the grass, a flower, your feet, and try to keep your attention there by not looking around. Then you might move to touch—feel the texture of wood, wool, cement, leaves, and so on. And then, taste—lick your arm, eat a berry. You don't have to do one sense right after the other without a break. You could focus on sight and then go for a little walk. Then when you come back, do smell, and so on.

Start with short sessions. As you settle into the retreat, you can extend the amount of time you spend on one sense and reduce the number of objects you focus on. For instance, first focus on visual awareness for twenty minutes and look at fifteen to twenty different objects. The next day you might spend twenty-five minutes focusing on three or four objects. By the end of the week you might be able to focus for an hour on only one object. But don't get ahead of yourself. Rather than forcing yourself into a straightjacket, gradually settle into a state of concentration and calm. You may not even notice it happening.

Retreat is mostly silent to provide the conditions to settle the mind. Don't worry so much about the internal dialogues or emotions that arise in your consciousness. Try as much as possible to rest your attention on whatever sense you are working with. You can repeat a word to yourself as a makeshift mantra. If you're looking at candlelight, repeat "yellow, yellow," or the roof, "thatch, thatch," as a way of keeping your attention from wandering too much. Try to keep to yourself and not look around because doing so moves you into mental chatter and away from your meditation object.

Latching Onto The Nipple

It's natural for the mind to flit from object to object and from state to state on a regular basis. Don't try to fight against that momentum. Just allow it to gradually slow down so that you become more still, more quiet, and more present in the moment. The mind also tends to comment about what it's meditating on. I encourage you to gently resist that tendency because once you allow the dialogue in, it takes you off into elaborate stories. Before long, you're daydreaming more than you're actually meditating. Don't be harsh with yourself though. Be as gentle as you can, as if your mind is an infant and you're lovingly guiding it to the nipple. If your attention wanders off, calmly bring it back. If you decide to change your visual object from someone's white blouse to the floor, try to do it with conscious intention. Say mentally, "I'm going to shift my focus from the white blouse to the floor."

What you want more than anything else is to be in control of your mind. Curiously, however, it's the one thing that tends to be completely out of your control. Most people are surprised to see how unsteady their minds are when they start practicing like this. You don't even notice as long as you get the things you like. But what happens when you don't? You're unhappy.

When you *do* experience bliss, you may not even notice how you got there. For instance, say you're walking down the trail and find a nice spot to sit and look at the lake. After a few minutes you become calm and clear. You haven't noticed your mood changing, but in a sense you've allowed the environment to settle the mind. However, it wasn't a conscious process. In meditation, what you're learning is how to *consciously* direct the mind to the wholesome. With practice, these states will be available to you at any moment, regardless of whether you're getting the objects that make you happy or not. This is mind training. At first it seems like such an effort. You might think to yourself, "Isn't it easier to just shift my attention to something I like?" When it works, it does produce a general level of happiness. However, because the mind has not been trained, anything can interfere with your good state—a harsh word from your partner, business not going the way you had hoped, the weather not cooperating, and so on.

By training your consciousness, you can create bliss wherever you go, whenever you want. You don't need your forest, your yoga studio, or your special friends; it's there for you always. This is the fundamental nature of freedom because those external objects are eventually going to be taken away from you by old age, sickness, decay, and death. On your deathbed, you're really going to be put to the test. Can you produce the bliss now?

Learning The Combination To The Lock

Let's put it this way. Suppose you're hungry and there's a lock and chain around the fridge. Some people in the room know the lock's combination but you don't. So you depend on those who know it to open the lock for you. The Buddha was called "a trainer of gods and men." Fundamentally, you should think of Buddhism as training—learning the combination—so that you don't have to rely on teachers or special circumstances to open the fridge for you. If you learn the combination, you are, in the words of the Buddha, "independent, clinging to naught in the world," and you can leave your teachers behind. The whole point of a teacher is to become redundant. And the whole point of the teaching is to become redundant. It's not to build a new identity as a Buddhist; the point is to become free.

Surrendering to the training isn't easy though, because it directly confronts your desire for control. Fundamentally, as an ego, your reaction to training is to say "No!" because you think that someone is trying to control you. For example, say you're sitting in meditation and the thought arises, "I'd like to go for a walk." And your little training voice pipes up and says, "No, you're going to meditate for fifteen minutes on a flower." As soon as you hear that voice, you get up and go for a walk. That's because your ego hears it as the voice of the parent. Any time you find yourself rejecting something that's basically in your best interest, you're reacting to your parents.

Teachers often get a lot of projections from their students about parental issues because they're telling students what to do. Hopefully, we can short-circuit this parental issue and go straight to the thing you really want to know, which is how to open the fridge for yourself. Everyone possesses the intuitive ability to learn, with training, to become calm and concentrated so that bliss arises. This is the first number of the fridge combination. If you can produce bliss at will, you're halfway home.

Why Do We Interrupt Bliss?

Focusing on the senses to access concentration and calm is a gentle and organic approach. If you don't allow yourself to wander off too quickly, the bliss will have a chance to arise. As it does, you now encounter another problem. What happens the minute you experience bliss? You panic. I've watched this in retreat after retreat over more than twenty years of teaching. After ten days, you are calm and concentrated, bliss is present, and inevitably you start chatting to a friend, which interrupts your good state. You actually *choose* the interruption. Why would anyone do that? Because of the fear of disappearing. If the bliss lasts for more than a few seconds, what you understand as "you" tends to dissolve.

For example, I might meditate for a little while, get into a blissful state, and then say to myself, "Hey, I'll go have a cup of tea." And I go and talk to good old Annie. I believe I'm still in the moment when in fact I'm not. Annie and I start talking about a yoga retreat she did in

Hawaii. I say, "Oh, I did a much better yoga retreat in Bali." And she says, "No, the yoga is much better in Hawaii." Then she thinks, "What does he know?" And I think, "What is she talking about?" Meanwhile, what has happened to our awareness of the present moment? It's gone! What has happened to our concentration? Gone! And our calm? Gone, gone, and gone. So we continue this pointless dialogue until it peters out, and Annie says, "I've gotta go." And I say, "Yeah, I've gotta go too." Then we run back to our meditation cushions to see if we can rebuild the bliss we lost.

The bliss I'm referring to isn't some vast feeling or some powerful Kundalini experience. It's much smaller—a very tiny, fragile egg. The purpose of meditation is to help you learn to reside in that quiet little moment of the now without getting distracted—no matter what.

Hello Bliss!

What "makes sense" of all the input coming from the senses?—the mind, which in Buddhism is considered the sixth sense door, the consciousness of something. It integrates and names phenomena arising from the five external senses. To illustrate, if the visual object is my face, then the mind labels it as "face." The mind can also have abstract objects such as love, fear, work, or relationship.

Like the senses, the mind door is also inherently blissful, but our thoughts, sensations, and feelings distract us from that bliss. If we get entangled in a thought, that thought will be the beginning of a conversation. Our ship starts to go back out to sea. One comment leads to the next comment, which leads to the next. In the process we've lost the initial recognition that both are blissful: that which is having the thought and the thought itself.

For example, at some point in your meditation your mind will slip back into the commentator's role, saying, "Oh, this is bliss." When it does, you are, in fact, distracting yourself from the feeling by labeling it. But by thinking instead, "That which recognizes the moment of bliss is also blissful," you aren't interrupting yourself, because you didn't let the labeling distract you; instead, you extended the bliss into the commentary mind.

So you come back to the bliss of the "now moment" again and again, whether it's through a sensing or mental object, by allowing consciousness to stay present with whatever is arising. However, if you lose awareness of the present moment, you lose your focus and start asking other people in the room for the combination to the fridge. These "people" are our pastimes, our work, our relationships—anything we depend on outside of ourselves to try to reach a state of joy. Sometimes it happens that our hobbies open the door to the fridge, or work opens the door, but that doesn't mean these things will work every time.

For instance, if you're meditating one morning on flowers in the garden and you become calm and focused, bliss arises. If you return to the garden the following day, bliss will not automatically arise, especially if you allow your attention to wander and your stories to take over. However, if you can stay fully present in every moment, with no attachment or aversion to the arising dialogues, then bliss not only arises, but can be maintained as well. Be careful not to fall back into the mind that rebels against the training, though, or goodbye bliss.

An important part of meditation is to accept when you're not feeling calm or blissful. In these instances, your job is to try to identify which particular monster has come along to distract you. It might be work, family, friends, physical pain, or conflicting emotions. Old arguments are great distractions. You remember something somebody said to you five years ago and then spend an hour going over it in your mind. Why would you waste time doing that? To make sure *you* are still in the game. This is why you interfere with bliss. You would rather be present in a less than wonderful state than risk not being present in a state of joy.

Leaving Retreat

Stepping outside of the containment field of retreat can also cause you to drop your state of bliss. This is because you have to communicate with other people again, and it may seem awkward to put on your social mask. Before retreat you could groove with everybody. Now, after four days in silence, you come out feeling great but feel somewhat disconnected with the outside world. With experience, however, you learn how to bridge both worlds—how to go back into your daily life and be yourself *and* carry the bliss with you.

Another reason people don't want to let go into bliss is that the rest of their world then begins to seem meaningless. This is a great spiritual trap. You come out of meditation and your inner experience seems to be all of reality, the entire universe. It seems difficult to return to balancing a budget, attending meetings, answering e-mails, and everything else in your life. The mistake is that you haven't learned how to apply what you learned in retreat to those everyday situations.

A retreat allows you to first calm your mind and establish concentration in the best possible circumstances—where you don't have to cook, clean, talk, or read. Then you learn to take it out of retreat. In daily life you need to master shifting your attention much faster while continuing to maintain the bliss. In retreat you can spend half an hour focusing on a purple orchid. When you come out of retreat, you have to gradually bring your functioning up to speed with the world. Within a split second, you need to be able to register purple orchid, black cat, blue sky.

Will The Neighbors Think You Are Weird?

The other major obstacle to carrying the bliss forward post-retreat is that you continue to take refuge in the happenings of your life, rather than in the immediacy of the present moment. Even though this is a false refuge, you would rather be chatting with someone than be in a clear state just sitting and looking out of the window. The reason for giving priority to social bonding goes back to a very early need, which is for the mother's love and acceptance. As children we are conditioned to fulfill mother's expectations and demands in order to get love. But now we are adults and that approval is no longer necessary. Still, as social animals our biggest need is to belong, and there's a very good reason for this—without other people we would die. We function as a pack. We're not as fast as the cheetah, as strong as the bear, nor can we see as well as the hawk. We know instinctively from birth that we cannot survive on our own. We rely on each other for our food, clothing, shelter, and medicine. That's why being approved of and accepted is often more important to us than being in a clear radiant state.

Interrupting Bliss On Purpose

Learning to consciously drop the bliss teaches you how to integrate it into daily life; it's a way to see how grounded you are in your practice: "Can I change the focus of my meditation from the purple orchid to the black cat and then back to the purple orchid without losing my blissful absorption?" This training will teach you how to interrupt bliss and still not lose the reins to your ego.

From the point of view of transcendent consciousness, the ego doesn't vanish when it enters a state of bliss; it is simply put where it belongs, which is *behind* the horse. The non-awakened consciousness puts the cart (the preference mind) *in front of* the horse (the bliss). When that happens, the cart doesn't go anywhere. All roads lead back to "me"—my life, my problems, my worries, me, me, me, me, me. However, if you put the horse in front of the cart, then no matter where the "me" goes, the situation is blissful. There is no situation that can distract you from the mind of clarity and bliss.

Your State Is A Precious Object

The awakening consciousness makes the decision—"I don't care if the social bridge collapses. I claim the liberated state as being more important than whether I live or die." This is fundamental if you want to dwell in the state of Buddha, or Christ, or whatever transcendent being you want to emulate. As a personality, you have limited appeal. Yet, if you put your refuge in the transcendent state, you become vastly more appealing (except to those people who are absolutely terrified of the dissolution of their boundaries).

The curious thing is that you don't actually lose yourself. As Jesus said, "Those who lose their lives for me will find them." In choosing the bliss state over who you think you are, you actually gain a stronger sense of self. But please don't make the mistake of thinking that I'm saying you should not be a social being. We *are* social beings. The question is, are your social needs controlling you? If they are, this signifies putting the cart before the horse. When things are in the right order, everything works better, including your social life.

When you sit down to meditate, just remember there is going to be a very strong desire to get up and go say hi to somebody, a very strong desire to get up and go for a walk or check the laundry. If you can manage to carry the concentration and calm from the meditation cushion to the laundry room, losing bliss won't be a problem. But if you drop it in order to get your laundry done, you've sold yourself to the devil. You have sold your birthright as an awakened being in order to be a temporary human being for forty or fifty more years. Let's face it—fifty more years and the whole story of your life will be irrelevant to everybody. A clear state, however, becomes a precious object of veneration that will be carried from lifetime to lifetime.

For more resources on the topic of establishing a solid meditation practice, visit planetdharma.com/dare/resources.

CHAPTER

10

NUTS AND BOLTS OF PRACTICE:
The four foundations of mindfulness

W E LIVE IN A HOUSE OF CARDS. This house comes tumbling down and liberation dawns when we learn to analyze our experiences and realize that no matter how fascinating, bewildering, or terrifying they are, they do not create an "I." The Four Foundations Of Mindfulness, which are the basis of all meditation practice, help us look objectively at ourselves. They break down our experience into four categories: bodily sensations, feelings, contents of mind, and overall mental states.

Curiously enough, liberation happens principally in the body. You can be liberated mentally and emotionally, but ultimately the body must witness it. For some, it starts as shaking, like earth tremors, then whatever holding patterns are locked within the body release. When that happens, you know that a deep body memory has been cleared. If the shaking returns, it's simply to clean up little corners of the tension that were missed. You may feel anxious or discombobulated by what's happening, but instead of distracting yourself from the uncomfortable feelings by saying to yourself—"Oh, I feel terrible. I'm going out to get a pizza and see a movie"—you sense that something is being revealed to you and so you stand your ground and wait.

The body is where all of our conditioning begins. Physical conditioning, such as cravings, chemical sensitivities, and allergies, is basically built in the first months of life—even *before* conception! If your mother had an adverse reaction to tomatoes, you might too.

Emotional conditioning is laid down from about one-and-a-half to five years of age. All your negative emotions are infantile; this is obvious from the way you respond when your buttons are pushed.

Mental conditioning is the biggest weapon of all. Your views are tenacious because they are your principal defense to keep the persona in place. You developed them between adolescence and early adulthood based on your set of social and cultural influences or your rebellion against them.

Obstacles To Your Liberation

Liberation is a process of "becoming younger and younger" to remove these layers of conditioning, like peeling an onion. The biggest obstacles are your views. Once you see through these, the repressed emotions are revealed. Once you get beneath the emotions, locked tensions in the body can be revisited and released.

As an example of the interrelationship between these layers of conditioning, say I believe I'm allergic to chocolate. This view may be hiding some negative emotional experiences in my past, such as the fact that my mother used chocolate to bribe me. So the present physical allergic reaction is built upon my relationship to my mother.

Like money in the bank, the more views you have, the less likely you are to go bankrupt. If one of them is overturned, you still have lots of others to hold your image together. However, if an interaction becomes too intense, you switch to an emotional defense. Have you ever had a fight with your partner? At some point, rationality flies right out the window, and you're both reduced to two-year-olds standing there toe-to-toe saying, "It's gotta be done my way! Say you're wrong! Tell me you love me!" And, if you win, you still lose because the other person is just going to get even eventually. They may submit in the moment and say, "Sure, you're right," but when you ask, "Want to go to a movie?" you can expect them to say "No!"

After one's emotional defense has been penetrated by awareness, the physical holding patterns in the body start to unwind. How strong the tremors will be depends on how threatened you felt in early childhood. It may seem like you're trying to tame a wild horse.

Acknowledge The Good States Too

It is very important to acknowledge positive states because recognizing them is what perpetuates them. This is the single biggest failing in most people's lives—when something good is present, they don't acknowledge it. Many times I've said to someone, "Well done! That's excellent!" and they answer unconvinced, "Oh well...you know...." Or I say, "That's a delicious cake!" and they say, "Well, it's just okay." But if I say, "That sucks!" they quickly agree, "I know, doesn't it? It's really terrible!"

Most people are in a neutral or good state ninety percent of the time. However, those negative states run like tropical vines through the rest of their lives. We don't trust the good because as children we were interrupted. Our mother needed to take us to daycare, for example, and disturbed our bliss. We didn't know what was going on; we just saw it as an interruption. Consequently, the first thought that comes up in our minds when we're in a state of bliss is "Aha! All right, where are Mom and Dad? What are they going to make me do now? Go to bed, get up, wash my face, put my toys away, do this, don't do that!" The way you were conditioned becomes your habits. The good news is that habits are only habits and can be broken if you're willing to apply some effort.

Riding The Dragon

It's also important to acknowledge when you're in a bad state. "Are you angry?" "No! I'm not angry!" "But you sound angry." "Well, I'm not!" Remember that the personality is built to defend itself and keep its shadow far from the light. First, acknowledge what's going on, and then change the label. Instead of saying, "I'm a bad person because I'm angry," say, "My heart is pounding and I'm sweating bullets." This gives you the freedom to "ride the dragon"—to ride the energy of unwholesome or unpleasant states of mind without going into reactive knee-jerk patterns. If you can shift your view in the moment, you will experience bliss and clarity. Rage will become the fire of love; confusion will become the light of wisdom; greed will become the generosity of the universe. If you can't trust that, you're stuck as a little persona floundering around in a sea of six billion other people scrambling to get their share. You choose.

Q: *Every time my daughter would leave to go back to college, we'd get into a fight. Do you think we were afraid of feeling the pain of separation, and fighting was a way of distracting ourselves from it?*

Rebelling is part of the process children go through to get ready to leave home. Your daughter would have felt guilty if she'd said, "I don't want to spend time with you anymore," so instead she picked a fight and when you became angry, she had a good excuse to leave.

Separation may seem like a rending, but it isn't painful if you change your perception. Rather than seeing it as a negative experience, imagine that you're sending a spore out into the universe to explore new worlds. It depends on how you look at it, doesn't it? Are you losing something or are you gaining something? Your daughter's enriching life experiences will benefit both of you in future times together.

Q: Shouldn't we recognize that pain is one of the realities of life?

You must first acknowledge the pain—assuming you get past being angry. Once you have, remove the label and just experience it as a dance of energy. Don't call the tears and shaking a bad thing. Call it a joyous display of the energy body—like an orgasm, or the mother of the bride crying tears of joy at her daughter's wedding. It all depends on how you label an event. Life is an endless series of separations; it's only the persona's resistance to this truth that creates suffering. When you accept its transient nature, then every moment is creation and dissolution. Then you can luxuriate in the bliss of the peony and also accept the poignancy of its passing.

Q: What about combining meditation with chanting? A friend taught me a chant, but it's a little fast and I can't understand all of it.

Well, you can slow it down. One mantra I suggest is *OM AH HUM*. Imagine a white light in the forehead, a red light in the throat, and a blue light in the heart. The white light regulates the body, the red light regulates communication and emotion, and the blue light balances the mind.

What do you say when you see something for the very first time? "Ohhhhh!" What happens when you see it for the second time? "Aahhh!" What happens the third time? "Hmm...." *OM* is discovery, opening the mind, like discovering a shortcut to work. *AH* is opening the throat;

it's a recognition of that discovery. For instance, driving on a parkway through the hills is better than navigating the traffic in the center of town. And *HUM* is understanding and integrating it: "Yep, this is my new route."

Dāna Means Generosity

The first *parami*, or "virtue," to develop on the path to enlightenment is generosity. Generosity communicates your trust in the universe. It's not just about money. It's also your time and energy, and your ability to engage emotionally with others. Exercising the generosity principle is saying, "I am strong enough. I am capable enough to take care of myself in the future, so now I can share." Giving is also a good way of letting go of past hurts. If you are angry with anyone, you can break the back of your negativity by simply asking them what they want and giving it to them. It is impossible to remain in a negative state toward somebody as you reach out to give them a gift.

There's resentful giving, like when you feel obligated to give to the church. But if you give of your own free will, you won't feel that way. Your sense of community will be much stronger too. Remember the barn raisings and sewing circles of the past? We don't have those now because people move around so much. To be generous today, you have a harder task because you have to practice random acts of kindness toward strangers.

For more resources on the topic of the 4 Foundations of Mindfulness, visit planetdharma.com/dare/resources.

CHAPTER

11

MAGIC CARPET RIDE:
Coming to trust

THE NUMBER ONE THING A TEACHER SEES IS RESISTANCE. At the bottom of your being there is a firm hand on the control dial: *"I don't think I agree with this. He seems like a good guy, but he sure is full of himself. I think he's just after my money. Oh, he wants my body."* Or, *"Wow, he's a fantastic human being. He has no faults of any kind. He's just amazingly wonderful...at least for now."*

What you resist is giving up your power to decide what the truth is. The teaching is not trying to take that power away from you—that would turn you into a zombie. What it does do, however, is make you aware of how relentlessly you seek control. Who holds the bottom line? Me, the ego. The "I" is the bottom-line decider of everything. Clinging to such a false sense of control is your ultimate form of resistance.

The hardest place to drop the need for control is in relation to other people. Why? Because the very thing you're resisting at the core is Mommy and Daddy. Your identity was carved by how you reacted to them interrupting you and telling you what to do; that's what the ego is. So when it comes to dealing with other people's attempts to dominate you, your reaction is based on the strategies you used with your family. If your mother was a talker, you might be a quiet resister. If your mother never said anything, you might talk non-stop or be equally quiet; both are possibilities.

In meditation your job is to see the pattern—not to fix it, not to get rid of it, but simply to see it. Awakening happens when you realize that there is nobody there except the resister who is controlled by aversions and desires. We avoid people and situations that we find difficult, even though they're our best teachers, because they show us where we get caught. Likewise, we cling to our objects hoping they'll somehow bring us the happiness we seek, even though they're temporary and unreliable. When we acknowledge how we get trapped in our patterns, we see how everybody else gets trapped too; this generates compassion.

Playing With Trucks In A Sandbox

Non-clinging awareness is the understanding that we are, by nature, one organism, one planetary consciousness with oodles of semi-independent satellites. It's only when we identify ourselves as living in separate bodies with unique personalities and histories that we try to control and manipulate others. But at the level of universal consciousness there's nobody directing the show because everything is perfect just as it is.

When an awakened being looks around, all he or she sees are awakened beings. Once you view people in this way, you don't need to resist anymore. All resistance is ego-based and egos are like little kids playing with trucks in a sandbox—"You ran over my truck! I'm gonna run mine over yours."

So the trusting process is a gradual understanding of our true nature.

However, this wisdom requires skillful means to put into practice. We must make distinctions. When a student enters the Dharma who's a potential Hitler, we assign him to weeding the garden under supervision—"Okay, pull those weeds there. No, no… those are the roses. Leave them alone." And when we meet a Mother Teresa we say, "Here are the keys to the city, please do as you like."

You can distinguish between different people's characters and still trust that at their core they are one field of consciousness that doesn't need direction or control. People become Hitlers because they feel weak. Others become Mother Teresas because they feel strong. What makes you strong is not being smart, clever, or sympathetic. What makes you strong, and therefore compassionate and wise, is blissful, clear awareness.

I once asked my guru, "Is trust awakening?" And his response was, "Complete trust is complete awakening." So who are you going to trust? It's a smart ego that takes twenty to thirty years with their teacher before they trust him or her. If a student trusts automatically, the teacher's job is to break that naiveté because it can be dangerous.

Q: *Where does the trust come from?*

The ego is never going to make the decision to awaken because it's afraid it will be obliterated. What actually happens is that you get so bored and tired of trying to control everything that at some point the depth of your being gives up. The consciousness gets so familiar with the negative building blocks of the ego that it stops trying to sustain it. In *Jodo Shinshu*, or Pure Land Buddhism, it is said that you cannot awaken through your own efforts, but instead must rely on Other Power, which is the transcendent consciousness.

The core of your being knows transcendence to be true. At some point there's a trust-based jump in consciousness that says "Okay." It's like you're on a magic carpet which gets pulled out from underneath you, and you drop through empty space and end up on the very same carpet. You end up exactly where you were before—awakened!

For more resources to extend your learning of the topics in this book, visit planetdharma.com/dare/resources.

Doug Duncan is a Buddhist teacher known for his energetic, insightful, and practical approach to paths of awakening. Known to his students as Qapel, Duncan has taught internationally for more than forty years, travelling and leading meditation retreats from Canada's Arctic to Mongolia, Bhutan, and Antarctica.

A Canadian born in Regina, Saskatchewan, Duncan began his journey to Achariya (Pali for "accomplished teacher") at the age of twenty-four as a student of Namgyal Rinpoche, to our knowledge the first Western incarnate lama, recognized by H.H. the 16th Karmapa of Tibet's Karma Kagyu lineage and H.H. Sakya Trizin.

Based on decades of practice and training with Namgyal Rinpoche, Duncan's teaching bridges the three vehicles of Buddhism–Theravada, Mahayana and Vajrayana–as well as the teachings of Western mystical traditions, psychology, art and modern science.

In addition to the teachings of Namgyal Rinpoche, Duncan has received teachings from numerous Tibetan masters, including H.H. the 16th Karmapa, the First Kalu Rinpoche, H.H. Sakya Trizin, Dilgo Khyentse Rinpoche and H.H. the Dalai Lama. He's thoroughly trained in the doctrine and practices of the Six Yogas of Naropa, Mahamudra, Dzogchen, the Abhidhamma, and the Western Divine Mysteries. He's also an excellent therapist.

In 1998 Duncan founded the Kyoto-based community named Dharma Japan. In 2005 he co-founded the Clear Sky Retreat Center outside Cranbrook, British Columbia, Canada with his partner, Catherine Pawasarat. In 2014 Duncan and Pawasarat co-founded Planet Dharma. Individuals and communities affiliated with Planet Dharma and Clear Sky teach and practice in the U.S., Canada, Japan, the U.K., Germany, New Zealand, Australia, Guatemala and South Africa.

Duncan continues to teach and lead retreats around the world at the request of students new and old.

ABOUT PLANET DHARMA

Dharma teachers Qapel Doug Duncan and Catherine Pawasarat Sensei are passionately committed to support beings who aspire to spiritual awakening in this lifetime, and to leveraging the power of that awakening to benefit all beings.

They believe that what's needed in our modern, Western culture are spiritual awakening practices that embrace both who we are and the modern culture in which we live.

To this end, Qapel and Sensei share four major approaches:

1. **Spiritual Awakening Through Action**

Since most of us spend most of our waking hours at work, we benefit tremendously by making our jobs a vocation, that is, our vehicle to benefit all beings.

2. **Spiritual Awakening Through Meditation**

Nothing beats meditation for learning to see how our consciousness works, and learning to choose healthier thoughts and emotions.

3. **Spiritual Awakening Through Learning**

The universe is an amazing, interactive campus. Being embodied means exploring and discovering. A joyful life full of wonder is one of the byproducts.

4. **Integrating the Shadow**

Funny how the parts of ourselves we've learned to reject have a habit of showing up inopportunely. We can accept and transform them so they become our greatest strengths.

Planet Dharma focuses on teaching and training methods that support you to transform outdated views into a more open mind, limiting habits into supportive ones, and conflicted emotions into healthy feelings. To these ends, this teaching emphasizes practicing both as individuals and in spiritual community.

The results? More joy, more creativity, more compassion, more true wealth and more freedom.

Visit planetdharma.com to find out how this path can work for you to transform your life into greater spiritual awakening in this lifetime, and benefitting all beings.

ABOUT CLEAR SKY CENTER

Qapel Doug Duncan and Catherine Pawasarat Sensei are the founding teachers of Clear Sky Meditation and Study Center, which is nestled in the foothills of the BC Rockies, Canada.

Clear Sky exists as a place of engagement for people with a heart for spiritual exploration who are looking for ways to awaken more quickly and deeply. Our purpose is to provide an outstanding container for practice and study for students from around the world.

Our key principle is that all growth and transformation happens within a stable container. Outer clarity supports inner clarity. If we are ever short on inner clarity, the outer clarity of a container can quickly restore our balance. We can unpack this into five principles:

1. **Honor your space.**

Have you noticed how you feel when you enter an environment that's beautiful, spacious and well-cared for? Learning how to create this for ourselves builds a strong foundation for our explorations and practice.

2. **Structure and routine are your friends.**

Consciously chosen structures and routines give us a tremendous amount of freedom and creativity, as well as the ability to form new healthy habits.

3. **Communication shapes the space where we meet.**

With conscious and skillful speech - and by being aware of our effect on the space - we can co-create a loving, honest and open container for deep connections to happen.

4. **Cleaning up big areas of your life frees up energy.**

Each time we bring outer clarity to a major aspect of your life we free up enormous amounts of energy.

5. **It's easier with others.**

That whole independence thing - it's an illusion. Especially when it comes to major shifts in our lives, we need the honesty and support of good spiritual friends.

Clear Sky's pristine property features a variety of beautiful natural landscapes, stunning views of the Rocky Mountains, individual meditation cabins, an innovative and organic food forest, green building and the benefits of years of ecological restoration and conservation efforts.

In addition to Clear Sky's own programming, like-minded groups and individuals are invited to contact us about booking your own courses and retreats. We are a registered non-profit organization with charitable status. Does our story resonate with you? If so, learn more and contact us through www.clearskycenter.org.

Listen wherever you get your podcasts!

DHARMA IF YOU DARE
A PLANET DHARMA PODCAST
with Doug Duncan & Catherine Pawasarat

Exploring the cutting edge of spiritual awakening

New Episodes Every Friday!

LISTEN. WE DARE YOU.

The following is an excerpt from Doug Duncan
and Catherine Pawasarat's bestselling book,
Wasteland to Pureland.

WASTELAND TO PURELAND

REFLECTIONS ON THE PATH TO AWAKENING

DOUG DUNCAN
AND
CATHERINE PAWASARAT

PRAISE FOR
WASTELAND TO PURELAND:
REFLECTIONS ON THE PATH TO AWAKENING

Wasteland to Pureland is a crystal clear guide to the many pitfalls, nuances, and puzzlements that can arise on the path to enlightenment. Authors Duncan and Pawasarat write from experience, offering the reader calm authenticity and heartfelt encouragement. Highly recommended for both fledgling and experienced travelers.

—**Dean Radin, Ph.D.**, *Chief Scientist, Institute of Noetic Sciences*

Catherine and Doug skillfully apply insights from their years of spiritual practice to the critical issues of modern life. Their book challenges us to explore what is truly needed to live a fulfilling life and to make a contribution that is larger than ourselves.

—**Susan Skjei, Ph.D.**, *Director, Authentic Leadership Center, Naropa University*

Wasteland to Pureland provides a priceless map to guide you to your Best Life through a practical, accessible and deeply enjoyable program of spiritual growth. Longtime Buddhist teachers Doug Duncan and Catherine Pawasarat have described a path that anyone can follow through the process of engaging spirituality with your life, your family and your work. Their path leads from your office to the stars and back, providing a limitless environment in which to fully engage with your life and your world. I can imagine returning to this book again and again."

—**Bryan Welch**, *writer, consultant, entrepreneur, longtime publisher of Mother Earth News, Utne Reader and many other magazines about mindfulness and sustainability.*

This wonderful book is a timely and welcome beacon of light and hope in a world increasingly consumed by chaos and darkness. Profound, yet filled with practical and grounded wisdom, Wasteland to Pureland is not merely a book, it is itself a journey that if followed, offers a clear path to liberation and awakening. This is a must-read guidebook for all spiritual seekers.

—**Deborah Price**, *Founder/CEO of the Money Coaching Institute and author* of Money Magic: Unleashing your Potential for Wealth and Prosperity *and* The Heart of Money: A Couple's Guide to Creating Financial Intimacy.

Continuing on the path of the great wisdom traditions, Doug Duncan and Catherine Pawasarat provide us with an invaluable contribution—relevant teachings placed within the contemporary crisis of our time. In these writings, we are given a map to negotiate the spiritual and the material, the inner and outer landscapes of our collective soul co-evolving here on this planet. As we arrive in this illuminated state called "the Great Healing," we discover that we can invoke awe, wisdom, and wonder to solve even the deepest challenges of our wounded world.

—**Lauralee Alben**, *Founder and CEO, Sea Change Design Institute*

Doug and Catherine have always touched me with the depth of their presence, wisdom, humility, and humor. All of them comes through as a clear transmission of deeper states in this book, and their descriptions of how to recognize, journey toward and enter into those deeper states are invaluable. This is not a book only for the mind, or for the body, or for the spirit, but all of them at once. In the world of spiritual literature, esoteric teachings can become dry and removed. Nope—this book is juicy!

—**Mark Silver, M.Div.**, *Master Teacher in the Shaddhulliyya Sufi Tariqa and founder of Heart of Business*

Reflection 4
Protecting Against Hurt Is What Hurts

Liberation through Letting Go

The feeling of hurt comes from the past. It can be transformed by feeling love in the present. To feel love in the present, the hurt must be let go.

It sounds so simple. But complexity arises because a network of habitual sensations, emotions, and thought patterns forms and, over time, calcifies around our self-protective reactions to past hurt. These, too, must be released.

Where, then, do we start on this path to love?

It starts with the body. If we can let go of the muscle tension related to the past experience of hurt, then emotional and mental models that have been bound up can also be freed. From the perspective of the physical body, letting go often appears as visible or felt phenomena such as trembling, shaking, or shivering. This indicates the release of the muscle tension that has been held, a de-armoring of the body, and a letting go of the hurt. This is a beautiful and important step on our way to greater love.

Such physical de-armoring happens on its own through the process of deep meditation. We can support this process of unfolding more quickly but sustainably through many different approaches developed over the last fifty years.[53] Emotionally and psychologically, we can take advantage of therapy, counseling, family constellations, and the like to release emotions held in the body. Physically, massage, yoga, traditional Chinese medicine, tai chi, and related therapies are very helpful.

Why let go? After all, each of us has good reasons to feel hurt. The key thing is, it's this very act of letting go that liberates us. And, since hurt is one inevitable aspect of life, we would benefit from letting it go again and again. Letting go is a skill that we can develop through deep meditation practice over years and through the methodologies described above. Modern approaches continue to emerge in different modalities, including reframing techniques and our *Going to the Core* exercise.[54] Imagine the amount of energy that becomes available to us when it is no longer tied up in hanging on to past hurts.

And the liberating journey continues. Once we get good at letting go, we let go of letting go. Then, we experience the liberation of *transcending*: it is a gerund, an active and continuous happening. After letting go of the emotional tension of hurt, we then allow the energy that was stymied by clinging to being hurt to then move toward forgiveness or other emotional release. Then, the mind's and heart's energies are opened up, and we can naturally embrace equanimity. Equanimity is another word for peace of mind and heart.

Now the former emotional tension is available to be transformed into creative tension.[55] When there is a gap between the

---

[53] See, for example, Alexander Lowen, *Bioenergetics: The Revolutionary Therapy That Uses The Language Of The Body To Heal The Problems Of The Mind* (London: Penguin Books, 1976), and Wilhelm Reich, *The Function of The Orgasm: Sex-Economic Problems of Biological Energy* (New York: Farrar, Strauss and Giroux, 1973).

[54] See more about how we use reframing and our *Going To The Core* exercise in Reflection 15: Only the Shadow Knows, under the subhead *Using the Shadow as a Resource*.

[55] Peter M. Senge, *The Fifth Discipline*, (New York: Currency Doubleday, 2006), 139-44.

4: PROTECTING AGAINST HURT

vision of how we'd like our life to be and how we experience our current reality, there is a lot of energy held as tension in the dynamic of that gap. We can respond to this gap with either emotional tension or creative tension. We tend to experience the former as stressful and the latter as a source of tremendous inspiration and motivation to action.

How do we make the move from emotional tension to creative tension? By making a plan and developing step-by-step actions that address the situation we can accomplish the transformation from one to the other. Depending on the situation, our plan of action may be a note to our self to, say, listen more and speak less, or it may be a more complex process involving input from multiple stakeholders.

Our emotions provide us with important information regarding energy and other blocks in the body: the body holds the tension, and the emotional tension manifests in tandem as a cover over the physical holding. To release tension and other energy blocks in the body, we often need to release the emotions first, and to do this, we must get past the stories, excuses, and distractions that the mind creates to protect and hide from the hurt and trauma itself.

One tactic we may use to hide is to pretend (and even believe) that there is no trauma. Often, we can't remember it because the emotions are acting as a layer of protection, blocking out the hurt and obfuscating the facts. So, we pay attention to the emotions, rather than the words or ideas. For instance, if Cheng feels hurt by Marguerite, he may feel inclined to recount all the reasons and stories of how she hurt him. The hurt he feels now is an elaboration of previous hurts, often from early childhood,[56] that we each carry and that get triggered whenever we feel hurt later in life. The stories we tell now actually obscure the earlier hurts which are the core of our current pain. If Cheng gets in touch with just his emotions here and now (and if we support him in this as friends bolstering his unfoldment), he has a better chance of unlocking the stored patterns of hurt. Once the emotion is released, then the body naturally begins to let go of the energy

---

[56] See more on this in Reflection 3, under The Four Deep Ego Fears.

blocks it has been holding to store that emotion. Our role is to bring intention to the process.

Our first and biggest trauma as an ego is the feeling of separation, of the vulnerability of aloneness. We first experience this around the age of two when we realize that mother and I are two, not one. Moreover, it becomes apparent to each of us as two-year-olds that mother is not under my control, and therefore, I experience my basic defenselessness with, naturally, some terror and even anger: hence the Terrible Twos.[57]

We've all had this experience, and thus, we've all been traumatized. We can also be sure that we will all experience some kind of trauma again in our lives. The degree and intensity may vary, but what's important to note is that the core issue with any trauma is the hurt of separation and the shock it brings. These are the basic feelings that cause us to shut down in an attempt at self-protection. Our journey to a more joyful life and relationships begins when we realize that this strategy simply doesn't work.

Freedom from Trauma

There are two main paths we can walk to arrive at an ongoing state of spiritual liberation and freedom from trauma: therapy and meditation. We believe that we need to embrace both of these paths together to make true breakthroughs to spiritual liberation.

While they can be helpful under some circumstances, we don't consider psychotropic drugs (i.e., hallucinogens) a path to effectively healing trauma in and of themselves. Although we've found that they can liberate the ego to some degree, they cannot liberate the organism, the body. Nor do we include forms of physical exercise. Though physical exercise is essential for holistic health and can release tension, it cannot release the *sources* of tension on its own.

Therapy, including body-based therapies, can reveal and even help de-armor the defenses around old trauma, which is of

---

[57] See Reflection 14: Spiritual Energy Traders for more on this important topic of ego formation in our earliest years.

4: PROTECTING AGAINST HURT

enormous significance. However, most therapy can only go as deep as ego awareness goes because most therapy takes place in the context of the ego's understanding. This can help free some of the trauma but not all of it. Some somatic therapies or dream work can work in realms where the ego is not in charge, but getting to the root of the traumas entails reaching back to the hurt that took place before we were two years old, before the ego was formed.

And *full* liberation requires going past the ego into spacious emptiness, the realm of the spiritually awakened. This involves the path of meditative practice. One of the things this path explores is what took place before our ego coalesced. This is one of the things that's meant by the phrase, "transcending ego." When we understand what happened to our being before our ego was in place, and how our ego has been shaped, then we have more choices about how our ego can function optimally in our daily life. In other words, our ego doesn't have to automatically interpret and react to every situation from its own limited vantage point, which is what non-transcending egos tend to do.

In our experience, to gain greater freedom from an overactive ego (often called "ego-clinging" in Buddhist philosophy) and from the associated trauma, a combination of both therapy and meditation provides us with the most tools and opportunities. Therapy helps us to dismantle and clear out old conditioned patterns that don't serve us well anymore. Meanwhile, the meditative path helps build a healthy, vibrant, and resilient being from the ground up. By "healthy," we mean one whose natural manifestation is loving-kindness and compassion and is naturally interested in the well-being of the whole of life.

Our teacher Namgyal Rinpoche posed that the ego typically experiences a few traumas in a lifetime and that each trauma typically gets triggered again three to four times—resulting in shock waves stemming from the original trauma—before the trauma is finally and naturally released. Each subsequent wave is a little less turbulent than the previous one, like ripples from a rock dropped in a pond, gradually dissipating altogether.

As a result, protecting against hurt and thus shutting down

one's life force in some way or another only serves to maintain the trauma and continues to reflect and manifest as feelings of separateness. It's why so many of us feel lonely, sometimes even in a crowded room full of people we call friends. The original separation trauma related to our mother is a leitmotif held in our body, emotions, and thoughts, and can be triggered at any time.

For example, if my mother was not a very physically affectionate person, and I now have a partner who is also not very physically affectionate, every time I feel unloved by my partner's infrequent hugs, caresses, or other kinds of touch, it's a trigger for feelings from infancy. That is, regarding this phenomenon of response to a lack of physical affection, I'm really in a (usually unconscious) relationship with my mother. My partner, in a sense, isn't even there.

The irony—or we could say karma—is that I have been attracted to a partner or partners who have the conditioning to not be very physically affectionate. My partner helps me to see what's required to learn to recognize my needs and figure out how to have them met. It may be good communication and mutual support with my partner or it may be learning to let it go.

Therapy and meditation practice help us learn to let go of the habitual patterns that have been laid down over a lifetime in response to the trauma. However, only the transcending state can overcome this feeling of separation completely because it gives us the strength to let go of the last bastion of our trauma: ego clinging.

We can think of our being as a series of concentric circles. In the outer rings are protective patterns, casual ones, becoming more defensive as the circles get closer to the vulnerable core of our being. At the center is our ego, the inner fortress, most heavily guarded when under threat. Through therapy, meditation, and other spiritual practices we describe in this book, we realize that the ego doesn't need protecting after all because it's merely a concept we've built to protect against trauma.

We could call the release of this protection the transcendence of ego clinging. Buddhist traditions refer to the experience as spiritual awakening, a.k.a. recognizing the non-self, or a lack of

4: PROTECTING AGAINST HURT

a permanent, inherent self. Instead, we clearly perceive that we are an amalgamation of patterns that have been conditioned by our environments, experiences, and choices. The accompanying mind-state and heart-state of non-clinging awareness is always clear, radiant, blissful, vibrant—and empty.

"Empty" is the best English translation for the Sanskrit word *sunyata*. This is not the negative emotional emptiness that causes us to feel things like "my life is meaningless," which is a state that's rooted in ego identification. (It's about *my* life and therefore *me*.) Instead, emptiness here refers to a full, joyous, spacious state of potential and possibility. It's a state that's available to all of us at any given time; all we have to do is choose it.

If emptiness is available all the time, then why do we hurt? We hurt because we feel alone, isolated, and insecure. This makes perfect sense: as egos, we *are* alone, isolated, and insecure. We need to get past the ego to get past the hurt.

There are many reasons to feel motivated about this. For one thing, when we feel hurt, we act badly toward ourselves and others. Similarly, if someone does us wrong, it's because they feel hurt. While retribution may seem just and necessary, ultimately, it only spreads and deepens the hurt. No amount of vengeance makes us feel good. As the saying goes, an eye for an eye only ends up making the whole world blind.

Moving Beyond Pain

To move past ego-bound trauma, we need to see our own reaction patterns and how we react when the hurt is triggered. These patterns are not so easy to observe, since by its very nature the ego protects itself. One way it does this is by keeping these patterns obscured. The ego is built on hurt, primarily the trauma of separation from mother. However, a tremendously powerful and amazing characteristic of the ego is that it can come to know its own pain. What's more, it can also do something about it.

How does this work? We know that the ego is able to cultivate self-awareness. It's also worth noting that we can be aware—for example of our surroundings—but not be self-aware. The reverse is also true, so cultivating both awareness and self-awareness is important. Self-awareness offers us vast power because it allows us to know we are separate, and also empowers us to transcend this separateness to experience unity. This feeling of unity is what we call "transcendent awareness."

We can use the metaphor of looking into a mirror. We need a mirror—something separate from our self—to see our own face. Our ego is akin to our face, and the mirror is like awareness; the image in the mirror is self-awareness dawning. The ego has the ability hold up a mirror to itself, to become self-aware.

Once we know we are separate—we know that there is a face, and it is separate from the mirror—we can consciously choose to override the separation and choose to see the unity instead. We can see the image, the face, and the mirror as one entity while still maintaining the ability to perceive the component parts. We have the power to see what we choose.

This is transcendent awareness. As far as we know, no other living creature has both self-awareness and the power to transcend that separate self to experience unity.[58]

---

[58] A number of animals besides humans—including great apes, Asian elephants, dolphins, rhesus macaques, and, curiously, European magpies—have demonstrated self-awareness through the mirror test which continues to evolve to broaden human ideas about self-awareness," according to Virginia Morell, "Monkeys master a key sign of self-awareness: recognizing their reflections," *Science*, Feb. 13, 2017, http://www.sciencemag.org/news/2017/02/monkeys-master-key-sign-self-awareness-recognizing-their-reflection.

However the jury is out on animals' capacity for spiritual transcendence as we don't yet have any data on their interior life. That said, it is an intriguing subject worthy of ongoing investigation, and we are very interested in the consciousness of the animals in our lives, and in supporting one another to explore the nature of consciousness.

Meanwhile classic Buddhist texts describe the six realms of existence—the god realm, jealous god realm, human realm, animal realm, hungry ghost realm, and hell realm—and maintain that spiritual awakening is only possible in the human realm.

4: PROTECTING AGAINST HURT

With self-awareness, with knowledge, we come to know the edges that arise out of separateness. We can only perceive something if we are able to stand apart from it to apprehend it: thus, knowledge requires a divide. Separation is both the innate state of the ego and one of its Four Deep Ego Fears.[59] The wonderful thing is that, once we resolve the ego fears by letting go of them, this separation is precisely what drives us to the Holy Grail of a human lifetime: spiritual awakening. The power of the fears of the ego comes from trying to ignore or avoid them; only by transcending the fears can we render them powerless.

Hurt is a reaction; love is a decision. Hurt brings paralysis or stuckness, while love offers us greater freedom.

One of the meanings of the Sanskrit word *karma* is *action*, referring to the law of cause and effect. The Sanskrit word *cetana* means *decision*. Buddhist philosophy holds that karma is cetana; actions are based on decisions, as is our karma. If we are just reacting, going in the same flow with the hurt, then we will only get more of the same hurtful karma we've had so far. By choosing love, we make a decision that leads to good actions, good happenings, and good karma.

As mentioned, we each have lots of good reasons to feel hurt, starting with that original separation anxiety, usually related to recognizing our separateness from our mother in our first years. That's an extremely painful experience. More good reasons to feel hurt pile up in our life as our individual ego bumps and jostles with other egos. Egos are driven to self-preservation and self-promotion, basically to protect themselves. Fortunately, egos are also driven to wake up!

If we know that our own suffering is an unavoidable part of life—this is the Buddha's First Ennobling Truth, after all: "Life

---

[59] We go into the Four Deep Ego Fears in more detail in Reflection 3: If You Want The Present You Have To Open The Box. Briefly, they are: abandonment (separation), annihilation, insanity, and being evil (a.k.a. being a bad person or doing bad things).

is struggle"[60]—we soon realize that everyone is in the same boat. We then see that our ability to transcend *our* personal suffering depends on us helping others transcend *their* suffering. Since we're all in the same boat, the boat only serves its purpose if we're all pulling in the same direction. Otherwise, it goes in circles and eventually tips or sinks. This is the wellspring of the spiritual life—raising up others and ourselves to a better way of being.

The origins of the word *spirit*[61] include "animating or vital principle" and "breath," so it has a feeling of vivacity and flow. Suffering is more like stagnation. In this sense, the self-interested ego is a form of dullness trying to maintain a protective status quo to avoid more hurt.

Another effective way to foster the transcendence of trauma or other hurt is to put things in perspective. We are not alone in our pain. We live and work and relate to others continually, and everyone is struggling with the same dilemma: do I choose to open up to love or to protect myself from further hurt? Our experience, in fact, co-arises with others' experience; we need others to find our place in this world, and they need us for the same reason. In other words, we're all interdependent.

So, when we make the decision to choose love over suffering, we help ourselves as well as others. This does not make us naïve or a Pollyanna. Letting go of hurt also empowers us to move into a better, more functional, and ultimately more successful state of being. When we let go of the trauma, and with it, ego clinging, we don't lose intelligence, memory, the ability to make a good living, relate to other people, or anything else. In fact, we gain. We gain the ability to meet the reality of any situation and respond accordingly. We also gain the heart of loving-kindness

---

[60] The second is that this struggle has a cause: craving. Thirdly, the struggle has an end. Fourthly, the end of struggle lies in the Eightfold Ennobling Path.

[61] According to https://www.etymonline.com/word/spirit: "mid-13c., 'animating or vital principle in man and animals,' from Anglo-French *spirit*, Old French *espirit* 'spirit, soul' (12c., Modern French *esprit*) and directly from Latin spiritus 'a breathing (respiration, and of the wind), breath.'"

and the mind of compassion. These are qualities of inestimable value, to ourselves as well as every being on the planet.

Take the case of an adult who was sexually abused as a child; we'll call her Maxine. Through much courage, therapy, diligent spiritual practices, and other inner work, Maxine has processed the pain of non-support and lack of trust, as well as the rage stemming from her history. Through cultivating non-clinging and loving-kindness (toward herself and others) she's found release, what we call spiritual liberation.

Now, when Maxine encounters sexuality in her own life, and even abuse in others' lives, she can meet these events as a compassionate supporter and empowerer, rather than as a reactive victim. She's turned her suffering into a source of hope and strength for herself and others.

We must be clear though: the pain and sadness Maxine experienced—that each of us has experienced—will never go away. We could say that our protected hearts of stone only grow softer from the rain of millions of tears. Each of us can find a place that transcends our hurt and sorrow and from where we can live and engage in beautiful ways. From this space, we're not only unhindered by our past experiences, but wiser and more compassionate due to our journey to overcome them.

Love vs. Misery: Love Wins

Our strength comes from confidence, and confidence is built on experience. We need to ensure that our confidence is growing in healthy ways, not eroding. If our experience says the world is a hard and difficult place and that we are in decline, then we adopt that perspective, that belief, and it will determine how we feel, think, and act. The messages we get from those around us also influence what we believe. Alas, modern media feeds us unlimited examples of difficulties and horror. There is a kind of unholy glee, an almost compulsive sado-masochism in narrating how terrible everything is.

There are many reasons for this, and they are all rooted in the Four Ego Fears. What we fear draws us as well as repels us. We're drawn to death and destruction in part because we know we must die and thereby be "destroyed." Significantly, we're also drawn to these things because we instinctively know that if we face our fears, we can transcend them. However, we have to consciously choose to make the considerable effort to do this. Otherwise, we are likely to stay in a limbo of ongoing anxiety.

Since we all read, watch, and repeat the same fearful messages to each other, it can build a group ethic of impending disaster. Though there are wonderful things happening every hour of every day, 24-hour news channels narrate a globe in constant crisis; is it any wonder that anxiety and depression are so widespread? We are being inured to misery and disaster as the norm, rather than being educated about it being a choice. Victor Frankl contributed enormously to our understanding of this when shared how he survived the holocaust by consciously choosing to find meaning in the experience. Similarly, while his country, culture, and people have endured more than a half century of persecution by the Chinese, the Dalai Lama has dedicated his life to promoting peace.

As these examples demonstrate, what good news it is for us that loving, buoyant states are far more powerful than negative ones. A good state can blow a bad state right out of the water, so to speak, or perhaps we could say that a good state liberates innumerable negative states. When we are in a good state, we are open, kind, generous, friendly, humorous, and fun to be with. Other people are drawn to us like bees to nectar. Not only do we feel better, but people around us do too. We also think better and interact with others in more positive ways. Additionally, we're more productive and efficient in our work.

In Sanskrit, *saddha* means both *faith* and *confidence*. By making better decisions than choosing to be hurt—in other words, by choosing love—we build the faith and confidence that are the bedrock of our ability to step beyond the ego to spiritual liberation. Hallelujah.

EXPERIENCE ALL OF THE *PURELAND*

If you have enjoyed this sample reflection, you can get the whole book from the following sellers:

Amazon.com: http://bit.ly/ePureland-Amazon

Amazon.ca: http://bit.ly/ePurelandAmazonCA

Amazon.co.uk: http://bit.ly/ePureland-UK

Barnes & Noble: http://bit.ly/ePurelandB-N

Indigo: http://bit.ly/ePurelandIndigo

www.ingramcontent.com/pod-product-compliance
Lightning Source LLC
Chambersburg PA
CBHW070738020526
44118CB00035B/1492